OXFORD

BUSINESS FOCUS

PRE-INTERMEDIATE STUDENT'S BOOK

David Grant
Robert McLarty

01 Making contact
Companies

FOCUS ON WORDS

1 Match the photos a–e to these companies.

1 a Japanese retail company ....
2 a French cosmetics company ....
3 an Italian food company ....
4 a Spanish telecommunications company ....
5 a German car maker ....

2 What type of company do you work for?

3 Work with a partner. Use a verb in B, and a noun in C to make sentences about the companies in A, as in the example.

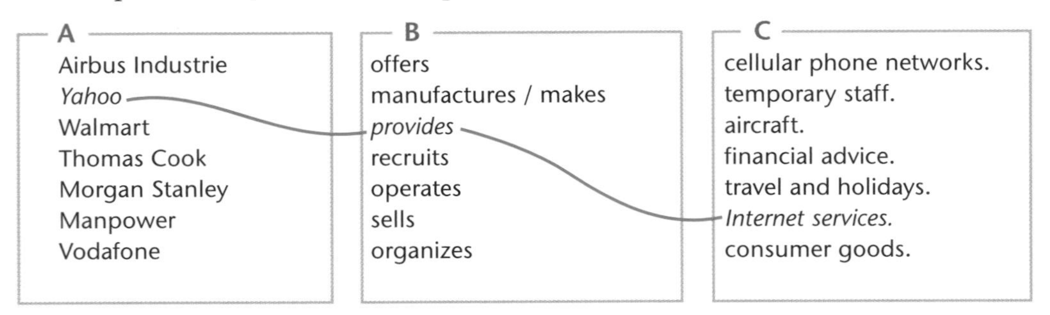

A	B	C
Airbus Industrie	offers	cellular phone networks.
Yahoo	manufactures / makes	temporary staff.
Walmart	*provides*	aircraft.
Thomas Cook	recruits	financial advice.
Morgan Stanley	operates	travel and holidays.
Manpower	sells	*Internet services.*
Vodafone	organizes	consumer goods.

4 Now make more sentences like those above about the companies in **1** and about other companies you know.

5 White goods are electrical appliances used at home, such as a fridge. How many white goods can you name? Which companies make them?

6 Read this company profile about the Italian white goods producer Candy-Hoover, and complete the text using the words in the box.

competitors	brands	head office	products
companies	turnover	employees	

With its 1 .... in Brugherio near Milan, Candy-Hoover is one of Italy's most famous 2 .... It is a family business with 6,700 3 .... and a large range of different 4 ...., such as cookers, dishwashers, and washing machines. Its 5 .... include Hoover, Rosières, and Iberna. The market for electrical domestic appliances is a very difficult one to be in and Candy-Hoover has many 6 .... in Europe and the Far East, such as Whirlpool, Electrolux, and Moulinex. Worldwide 7 .... is about $470 million with 80% of sales in Europe.

7 1.1 You are going to hear an interview with a Candy-Hoover employee. Listen and check your answers for **6** above.

8 1.1 Listen to the interview again and complete these questions.

1. Who .... you ....?
2. Where .... you ....?
3. What .... the company ....?
4. Do you .... any famous ....?
5. Is the electrical domestic appliances .... difficult?
6. How .... of that turnover .... in Europe?

9 Work with a partner. Take it in turns to ask and answer questions 1–4 in **8** about your company.

KEY WORDS

brand competitor consumer employee employ head office manufacture operate organize product provide recruit sales sell turnover

FOCUS ON GRAMMAR: Present simple and present continuous

1 Work with a partner. Ask and answer these questions.

1 What are the most popular clothing retailers in your country?
2 What makes a clothing retailer successful?
3 Are you wearing anything from these stores today?

2 Read this article and underline the correct form of the verb in *italics*.

GAP

Gap Inc. is a hugely successful clothing company. Founded in San Francisco in 1969, it [1] *operates / is operating* over 4,200 stores in the United States and five other countries and this number [2] *increases / is increasing*.

Worldwide, Gap Inc [3] *employs / is employing* 165,000 people. They [4] *sell / are selling* products under three main brands: Gap, Banana Republic, and Old Navy. All three brands [5] *do / are doing* well at the moment despite difficult economic conditions.

They spend a lot of money on advertising and the Gap name is now one of the most famous in the world. The company [6] *wants / is wanting* to expand in its present markets: France, the UK, Japan, Canada, and Germany, rather than go into new countries. Customers in other countries use the Internet. At this moment, thousands of customers [7] *buy / are buying* clothes at Gap's online stores. Gap's success over the last thirty-five years [8] *shows / is showing* the importance of the youth market in international economics. ■

KEY GRAMMAR

We use the *present simple* to talk about a habit or permanent state / condition.
Worldwide, Gap Inc. ***employs*** *165,000 people.*
We use the *present continuous* to talk about an event that is happening now.
All three brands ***are doing*** *well at the moment.*
Note that we can also use the *present continuous* form to talk about future arrangements.
I ***am meeting*** *him at 5 o'clock tomorrow.*

For more on the present simple and present continuous, see Language reference page 114.

3 Work with a partner. Ask and answer questions about Gap Inc. using these prompts, as in the example.

How many stores does Gap Inc. operate?

1 How many stores / Gap Inc. / operate?
2 This number / increase?
3 How many people / Gap Inc. / employ?
4 Where / operate stores?
5 They / spend a lot on advertising?
6 Where / thousands of customers / shop?

4 (((1.2))) Listen to an interview with some people who work for another international clothing retailer and complete this table.

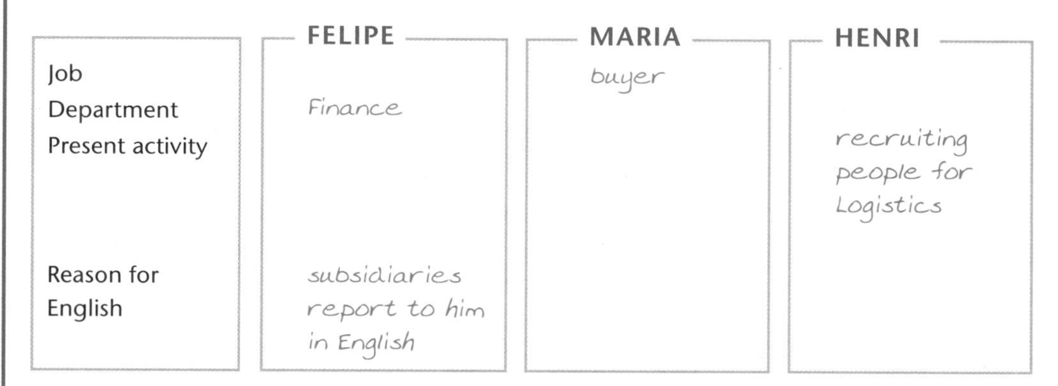

	FELIPE	MARIA	HENRI
Job		buyer	
Department	Finance		
Present activity			recruiting people for Logistics
Reason for English	subsidiaries report to him in English		

5 Work with a partner. Student A, turn to File 1 on page 84. Student B, turn to File 1 on page 92.

6 Silvia Riva is at a conference in the US. She meets another delegate, Tom Wilkes.

1 Complete the questions and answers as in the example.

2 (((1.3))) Listen and check your answers. Then, work with a partner and practise the dialogue.

3 Practise the dialogue again, but answer for yourselves, as in the example.

A *What do you do, (B's name)?*

B *I'm a research engineer. What about you?*, etc.

7 Work with a partner. Ask each other questions on these topics.

- Where you live
- Your hobbies
- Present projects
- Reasons for learning English
- Your cars

WORDS
Company facts and activities

GRAMMAR
Present simple and present continuous

EXPRESSIONS 1
Making and responding to requests

EXPRESSIONS 2
Getting through on the telephone

COMMUNICATION
Getting information on the telephone
Emails requesting information

BUSINESS ISSUES
Making good business contacts

END-OF-UNIT QUIZ

FOCUS ON EXPRESSIONS 1: Making and responding to requests

1 Do you prefer speaking to people face-to-face or on the telephone? Who do you talk to on the telephone? What problems do you have on the telephone?

2 Look at these questions and decide if they are said on the telephone (*T*) or face-to-face (*F*).

1 Could you ask her to ring me later, please? ....
2 Sorry. It's a bad line. Can you say that again? ....
3 Excuse me. Could you tell me the way to room 3421, please? ....
4 This is Sarah James. Can I speak to Mr Thomas, please? ....
5 This is Alison in Sales. Can you give me some details on the CC40, please? ....
6 Excuse me. Can you tell me the time? I have to leave at 6 o'clock. ....
7 Could you give me a hand with this filing, please? I'm really busy. ....
8 Can I have another coffee, please? ....

3 1.4 Listen to these responses a–h and match them to the requests in **2**.

4 What would you say in these situations? Work with a partner and role-play each situation. Your partner should respond, as in the example.

1 **A** *Sorry, it's a bad line. Can you say that again, please?*
B *Certainly. I'm calling from WPT.*

1 On the telephone you can't understand the speaker.
2 After a presentation you want the speaker to give you more information.
3 You want a colleague to go to the canteen and get you a coffee.
4 On the telephone you want the person to take a message for you.
5 At the canteen you have forgotten your wallet. Ask a friend to lend you some money.
6 You need your manager's signature on a document.

KEY EXPRESSIONS

Requests: *Could you do something for me, please? Can you help me, please? Can I use your phone, please?*

Responses: *Yes, of course. Sure. Certainly. Sorry, I'm afraid I'm busy. I'm afraid I can't. I'm afraid not.*

FOCUS ON EXPRESSIONS 2: Getting through on the telephone

1 1.5 A business journalist is writing an article about fitness centres. He telephones Life Health Clubs to arrange an interview. Listen to the conversation.

a Where is the Marketing Director?
b Why can't he speak to the Sales Director?
c Who does he finally speak to?

2 1.5 Work with a partner and try to complete this chart with the words used in the dialogue. Listen and check, then practise the dialogue with your partner.

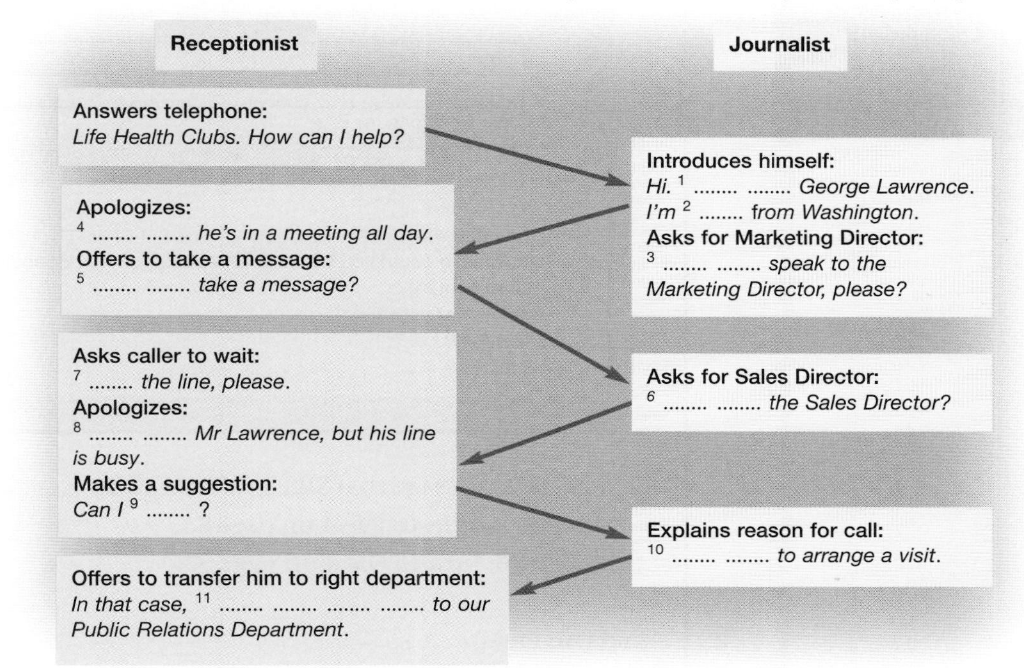

3 Match the telephone expressions in A with the responses in B. They are from different telephone conversations.

A		B	
1	Could I speak to William, please?	a	OK. I'll hold.
2	I'm afraid the line's busy.	b	This is Piers Olsen.
3	Could you spell that, please?	c	Can I leave a message?
4	Can I take a message?	d	Yes, speaking.
5	Sorry, she's away today.	e	Yes, of course. I'll put you through.
6	Hold the line, please.	f	Yes, please. Could you tell him ...?
7	Who's calling, please?	g	OK. I'll call back in a few minutes.
8	Is that Donna?	h	Certainly. It's T-H-O-M-P-S-O-N.

4 Work with a partner. Have telephone conversations. Student A, turn to File 2 on page 84. Student B, turn to File 2 on page 92.

KEY EXPRESSIONS

Can I speak to (name)? This is ... I'm calling from / about ... Can I leave a message? I'll call back later / tomorrow. Who's calling, please? Hold the line. I'll put you through. I'm afraid she's out / away / on the other line. Can I take a message? Could you spell / say that again, please? I'm afraid the line's busy / engaged.

FOCUS ON COMMUNICATION

1 Work with a partner. SVS is a recruitment agency based in Brussels. Student A works for SVS. Student B is looking for a new job. Student B sends this email to SVS.

1 Read the email.
2 Student A telephones Student B for more information. Student A, turn to File 3 on page 85. Student B, turn to File 3 on page 93.

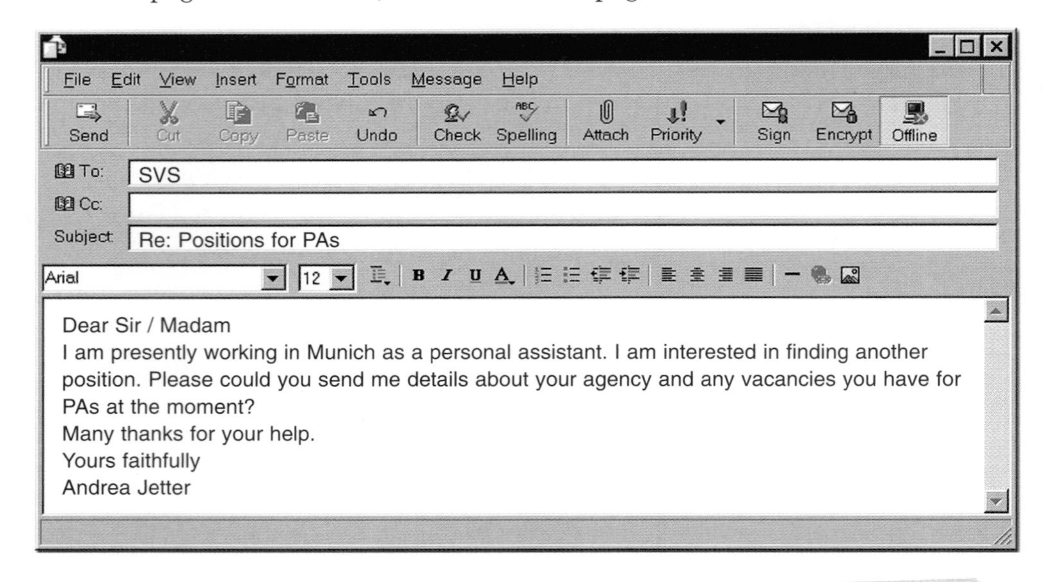
To: SVS
Cc:
Subject: Re: Positions for PAs

Dear Sir / Madam
I am presently working in Munich as a personal assistant. I am interested in finding another position. Please could you send me details about your agency and any vacancies you have for PAs at the moment?
Many thanks for your help.
Yours faithfully
Andrea Jetter

3 Read this message that SVS left for Andrea.
Student A, turn to File 4 on page 85.
Student B, turn to File 4 on page 93.

Please call SVS in Brussels re vacancy for PA.

2 Read this email.

1 How many requests does the writer make?

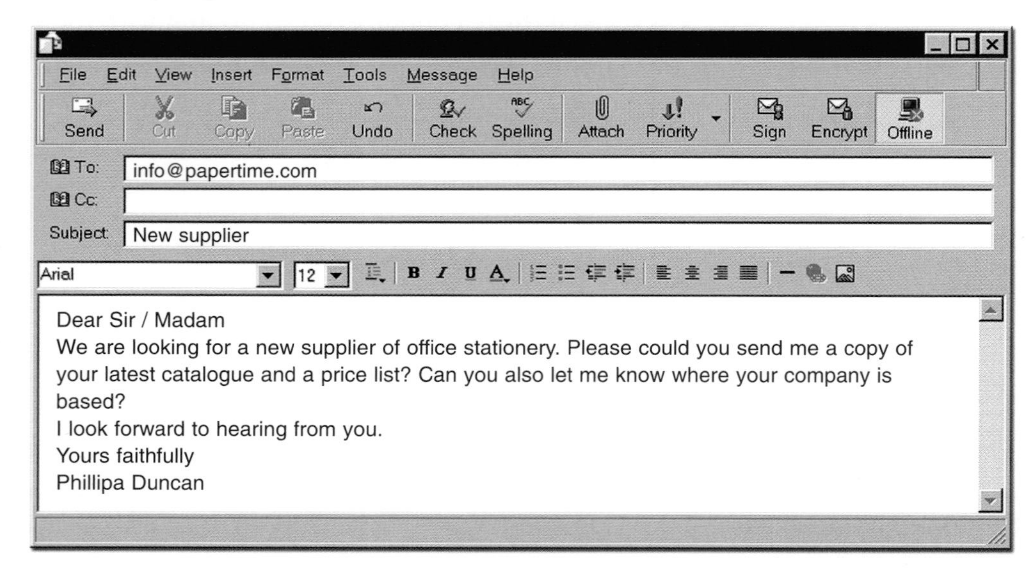
To: info@papertime.com
Cc:
Subject: New supplier

Dear Sir / Madam
We are looking for a new supplier of office stationery. Please could you send me a copy of your latest catalogue and a price list? Can you also let me know where your company is based?
I look forward to hearing from you.
Yours faithfully
Phillipa Duncan

2 Write similar emails to request information from:
- a training company (type and cost of courses / where)
- a company you are planning to visit (best time to visit / directions).

FOCUS ON BUSINESS ISSUES: Making good business contacts

1 Work with a partner and answer these questions.

1 How does your company get new business? Think of five ways.
2 How does your company stay in touch with regular customers?
3 How do companies stay in touch with you as a customer?
4 How do you find out about companies you want to do business with?

2 1.6 Listen to two colleagues and note down what they are doing to make contact with new customers.

3 Look at this extract from *The Bible of Business*. Work with a partner and think of a pro (positive thing) and a con (negative thing) for each point, like this: *Regular calls help to build good relationships with customers* (pro) *but they take a lot of time* (con).

How to make good contacts

- Make regular calls to all your customers.
- Keep your database up to date.
- Inform all customers about new products.
- Get regular feedback from your customers.
- Have an interesting website.
- Invite customers to events regularly.
- Maintain good advertising.
- Have a good PR policy.

END-OF-UNIT QUIZ

This is the end of Unit 1. Try this quick quiz to make sure you have understood everything.

1 What are these words?
   a a company's total annual sales: *t*................................
   b people who work for a company: *e*................................
   c to make something: *m*................................
2 What do these companies do?
   a Ford
   b Pirelli
   c Hoechst
   d Carrefour
3 Choose the correct sentence.
   a My firm is employing fifty people.
   b My firm employs fifty people.
   c My firm have fifty people.
4 Write the questions for these answers.
   a I'm working on a new project.
   b Certainly. It's P-L-E-double T.
   c We offer financial advice.
5 At a restaurant you would like to pay. What do you say to the waiter?
6 A person on the telephone is speaking very quietly. What do you say?

02 Sharing information
Products and services

FOCUS ON WORDS

1 Why do companies create new products and services?

2 2.1 You are going to hear an interview about the launch of EZ Squirt (said 'eeezeee'). Listen and decide if the following statements are true (T) or false (F).

1 The idea came from the research team. ....
2 They chose the name 'EZ Squirt' to attract kids (children). ....
3 They produced and tested seven different types of bottle. ....
4 It sells for the same price as normal ketchup. ....
5 It has more vitamins than normal ketchup. ....

3 2.1 Complete the flow chart for the development of EZ Squirt with the words in the box. Then, listen to the interview again and check your answers.

launch product	test design	brand product
cost product	do product research	trial product

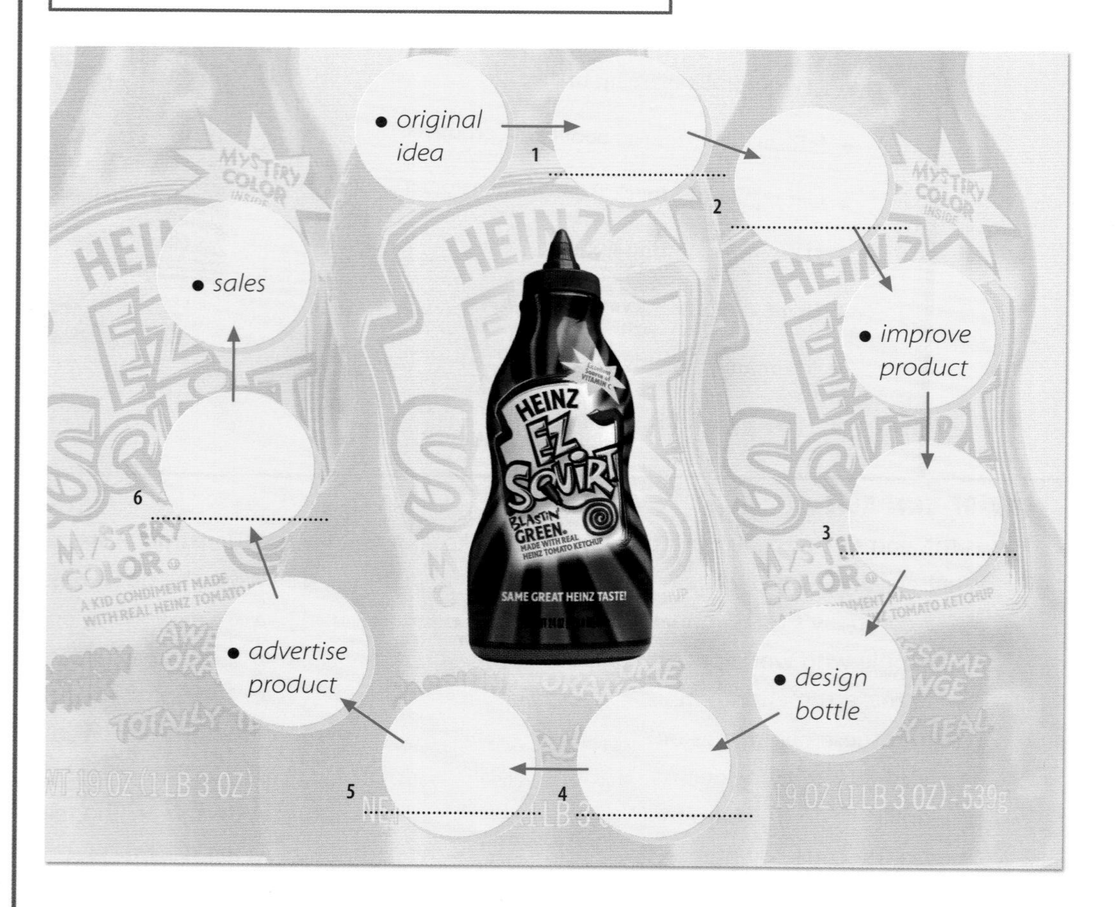

4 What are the stages in the life of your products or services? What stages are you and your department involved in?

5 Match the definitions in A to words in B.

A		B	
1	choose a name for a product	a	launch
2	promote a product to the public	b	do research
3	ask the public what they think of a product	c	brand
4	calculate the price of a product	d	trial
5	the way a product looks	e	cost
6	test a product	f	advertise
7	introduce a new product to the market	g	design

6 Read this article and complete the gaps using words in **3**. Sometimes you need a different form of the word, for example: *launch* → *launched*.

When you think about Heinz you probably think of tomato ketchup, the red sauce all children (and many adults!) seem to love to put on their food. Now there is purple, yellow, or even green ketchup! Heinz had the [1] original idea for different coloured ketchup after asking children and parents about their products. The tests showed that children wanted different colours and their parents wanted less mess! This was a big project for the [2] .... & Development people at Heinz. To make the sauce easier to pour they [3] .... a new bottle which was smaller, easier to hold and had a new type of cap. They [4] .... roughly ten prototypes before deciding on the final size and shape. The name is also easy for children to remember, 'EZ Squirt' (said 'eeeezeeee'), although Heinz might use different names in other countries. They [5] .... the new sauce in autumn 2000 and initially sales were very good. '4–12 year olds are our best customers', said a spokesperson for Heinz. 'We want the kids to have their own [6] .... – adults will continue to use the red ketchup. It is not exactly the same sauce – it tastes exactly the same but the children's version has added vitamin C. It also [7] .... 20% more than standard ketchup!'

7 Work with a partner and ask and answer these questions.

1 What new products or services does your company have? When did it launch them?
2 How does your company research and test new products?
3 How does your company advertise new products or services – online, in the press, or using other media?
4 How do companies attract public attention for a product launch? Can you think of any examples?

KEY WORDS

be involved in something   a brand   to brand   cost   design   a development process   do market research   do product trials   launch   promote   sell   sales   a stage   test a product   trial

WORDS
Development of products and services

GRAMMAR
Past simple

EXPRESSIONS
Starting a conversation
Keeping a conversation going

COMMUNICATION
Small talk game
Emailing a report

BUSINESS ISSUES
Successful brands

END-OF-UNIT QUIZ

FOCUS ON GRAMMAR: Past simple

1 Some product brands are so famous their names enter the language. Do you know what these ones are? Can you think of any others in your own language?

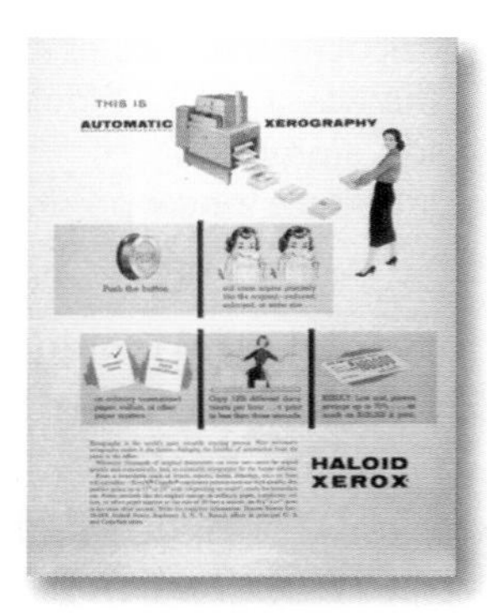

2 Xerox is one of the most famous companies in the world. Look at this chart showing some of the key dates in its history and answer the questions below.

1906	The Haloid Company was founded in NY. It manufactured and sold photographic paper.
1938	Chester Carlson made the first xerographic image in his laboratory.
1942	Carlson received a US patent for electrophotography.
1947	Haloid bought a licence to use electrophotography.
1948	Haloid trademarked the word 'xerox'.
1956	Haloid formed a joint venture with Rank called Rank Xerox Ltd.
1959	Xerox launched the first automatic, plain-paper office copier.
1960	Xerox opened a research centre in Webster, NY.

patent: the legal right to be the only person / company to make or sell a product or invention
trademark: a name or symbol (™) that is the property of a particular company and is not for public use

1 What did The Haloid Company manufacture?
2 Where did Carlson make the first xerographic image?
3 When did he receive the US patent?
4 What did Haloid buy in 1947?
5 When did they launch their first automatic copier?
6 Where did they open a research centre?

KEY GRAMMAR

The past simple of regular verbs like *launch* and *open* is formed by adding *-ed*.

*They **launched** the new product in San Diego.*

The past simple of many common verbs like *buy* and *make* is irregular.

*I **bought** a new photocopier for the office.*

We use the auxiliary verb *did* + base form of the main verb to form questions.

***Did** you **open** a new shop last year?*

For more on the past simple, see Language reference page 113.

3 Work with a partner to complete the next part of the Xerox history. Student A, turn to File 5 on page 85. Student B, turn to File 5 on page 93.

4 2.2 Listen to this interview and complete the sentences.

1 In 1988 Xerox .... their 2 millionth photocopier.
2 In 1994 they .... a new logo – the red X.
3 In 1998 they .... plans to open a call centre in Dublin.
4 In 2000 they .... a major sponsor of the Olympic Games in Sydney.
5 In 2002 a woman .... Chairman of Xerox for the first time.

5 Use the information from **2** and **4** to make questions for these answers.

1 It manufactured and sold photographic paper.
2 In 1988.
3 The word 'xerox'.
4 The Olympic Games in Sydney.
5 With Rank Xerox Ltd.

6 The mouse is one of the great inventions of the last forty years. Read this article and complete it with the past simple of the verbs in the box.

need	develop	have	require	launch
decide	be	demonstrate	spend	see

Great inventions

IN THE EARLY 1960s an American named Douglas Engelbart [1] .... the idea of combining the screen, the keyboard, and a type of hand-held controller to make computers easier to use. He [2] .... his invention at a trade fair in San Francisco. His mouse [3] .... a large wooden object with three buttons. It [4] .... six months' training to use it!

In the 1970s Xerox [5] .... the idea and in 1973 the company [6] .... the prototype of the world's first personal computer, the Alto. Steven Jobs, the founder of Apple Computers, [7] .... this machine in action in 1979 and [8] .... that his own new product, the Macintosh, [9] .... a mouse. A team of designers and engineers then [10] .... eighteen months creating the perfect mouse. It had one button, was the size of a child's hand and cost about $15 to manufacture. Today there are billions of them in action all over the world.

7 Think of another famous product and write a similar short article.

8 Write down five key dates in your life. Discuss them with a partner and exchange as much information as possible, as in this example.

1966 **A** *I moved to the USA in 1966.*
B *Why did you move there?*
A *My father got a job in Chicago.*

FOCUS ON EXPRESSIONS: Starting a conversation

1 Is it easy for new employees to get to know people in your company? What do you say when you meet a new person at work? What questions do you ask when you meet new people socially?

2 2.3 Listen to these conversations. Are the people meeting for the first time? Write *yes / no*.

1 Conversation 1 .... 2 Conversation 2 .... 3 Conversation 3 ....

3 2.3 Listen to conversations 1–3 again and answer these questions.

1 When did Tanja start? Where does she work?
2 Where are Michael and Graham? What does Graham offer to do?
3 Who do Tony and Hanni work for? Where did they first meet?

4 2.3 Complete these extracts from the dialogues, then listen again to check your answers.

1 A Excuse me? .... seat ....?
B Yes, sure. .... first day?
2 C .... know .... people ....?
D Not really.
C In that case, ... introduce .... some people. Come on!
3 E Your face is familiar. .... met?
F Yes. .... we have.

5 In making conversation we often use questions with *how*. Look at the answers in *italics* then complete these questions with words in the box.

often long old far many

1	How .... are you here for?	*Just two days.*
2	How .... is your company?	*It was founded in 1990.*
3	How .... people do you employ?	*About 350.*
4	How .... do you come here?	*About twice a year.*
5	How .... is your company from Madrid?	*Oh, about 50 km.*

6 Work with a partner. Start conversations using the information in the files. Student A, turn to File 6 on page 86. Student B, turn to File 6 on page 94.

KEY EXPRESSIONS

Is this your first day? Are you new? Do you know many people here? Nice / pleased to meet you. Nice to meet you too. Let me introduce you to … Have we met? Your face is familiar.

7 What topics do you like talking about at a business lunch or when you meet colleagues from a different country?

1 Look at the list below and tick (✓) your favourites. Add any others.

– cinema	– family	– travel ....
– food	– sport	– news ....
– books	– politics	

2 Are there any topics you would *not* discuss? Make a list.

8 Work with a partner. Brainstorm questions you could ask to start the conversation on the topics above, as in the example.
What kind of films do you like?

9 2.4 Listen to these conversations. Which topic in **7** is being discussed?

1 Conversation 1 .... 3 Conversation 3 ....
2 Conversation 2 .... 4 Conversation 4 ....

10 2.4 Listen again. How does the speaker usually open the conversation – with an information question (*wh-*) or with a *yes / no* question? Work with a partner and think of opening questions for the other topics in the list.

11 It is important to sound interested and ask logical questions in a conversation.

1 Look at the comments people are making in the cartoon. Choose a response from the box to show your interest, then ask a follow-up question, as in the example.

A *I'm a sales rep.*
B *Oh, are you? Do you travel a lot?*

Are you?	Is it really?	Wow!	Me too.
Did you?	Me neither.	Do you?	

a I'm a *sales rep.*
b My company's *Spanish.*
c I have *six children.*
d I love *pasta.*
e I worked *in the USA for three years.*
f I don't like *football.*

2 2.5 Listen to the conversations and compare your answers.

12 Start each conversation with the same phrases again, but this time replace the words in *italics* in the cartoon with information about yourselves.

KEY EXPRESSIONS

Do you like … ? *What about you?* *What's it like?* *Really?* *Me too / neither.*

WORDS
Development of products and services
GRAMMAR
Past simple
EXPRESSIONS
Starting a conversation
Keeping a conversation going
COMMUNICATION
Small talk game
Emailing a report
BUSINESS ISSUES
Successful brands
END-OF-UNIT QUIZ

FOCUS ON COMMUNICATION

1 Play this game with a partner. Student A starts in any column at the top and finishes at the bottom. Student B starts in any row on the left and finishes on the right. Use a counter. Move your counter to the next square when you ask or answer the question or respond correctly.

- If you land on the square that says, for example, *Have we met?*, answer the question: *Yes, your face is familiar. / No, I don't think so.*
- If you land on a square that says, for example, *In 1998*, say what was said just before: *When did you visit China?*

You must cross the grid without making a mistake. If you make a mistake, start again in any column at the top or in any row on the left.

STUDENT A START HERE

STUDENT B START HERE

Have we met?	In 1998.	Really!	When did you get here?	Me too.
About 30 km away.	Is this your first day?	Nice to meet you.	Yes, I did.	When did you join the company?
What time did you arrive?	When did you start learning English?	Where do you work?	Are you new here?	Twice a week.
One week ago.	Do I know you?	In 2000.	Do you know many people here?	Last night.
Me neither.	How often do you travel abroad?	About twenty minutes by car.	Detective novels.	How did you get here?

STUDENT B YOU HAVE WON!

STUDENT A YOU HAVE WON!

2 Read this email. Who is the message for? Why did the sender write it?

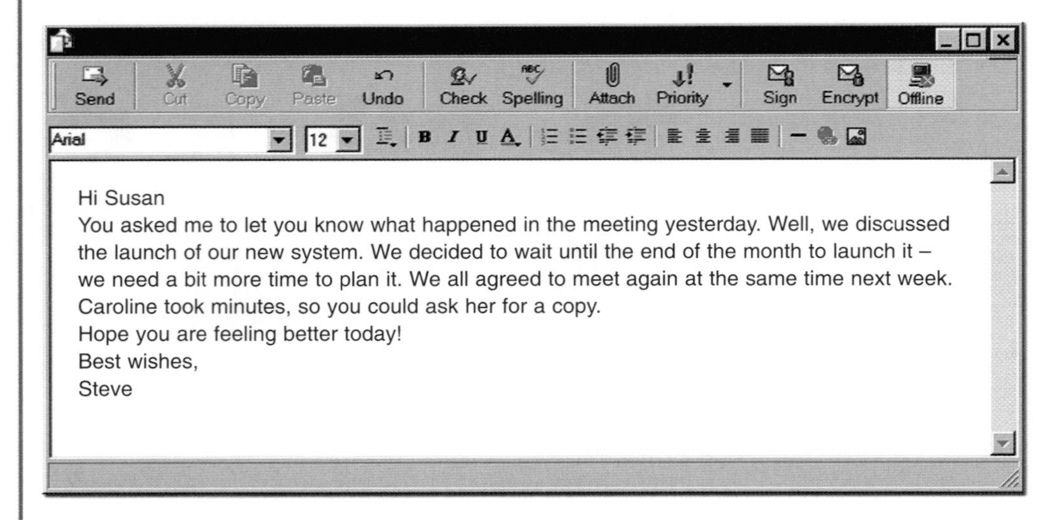

Hi Susan
You asked me to let you know what happened in the meeting yesterday. Well, we discussed the launch of our new system. We decided to wait until the end of the month to launch it – we need a bit more time to plan it. We all agreed to meet again at the same time next week. Caroline took minutes, so you could ask her for a copy.
Hope you are feeling better today!
Best wishes,
Steve

3 Work with a partner and write a similar email to tell them about the last meeting you attended.

FOCUS ON BUSINESS ISSUES: Successful brands

1 A recent survey named the three most valuable brands in the world as a drinks company and two IT companies. Can you name the companies? Which country are they based in? Check the answers at the bottom of this page.

2 2.6 Listen to this discussion between two people talking about brands.

1 What brands are mentioned in the conversation?
2 Why does she prefer to buy branded products? Do you agree?

3 Work with a partner and tell them what brands of these products and services you buy and why (think about advertising, reputation, packaging, price, etc.).

- food
- clothes
- coffee or tea
- computer software
- travel services and holidays
- beauty products and toiletries
- sportswear
- bank services

END-OF-UNIT QUIZ

This is the end of Unit 2. Try this quick quiz to make sure you have understood everything.

1 Put these verbs in the past simple form.
   a do ....
   b make ....
   c sell ....
   d buy ....
   e think ....

2 Find other ways of saying these words.
   a launch ....
   b manufacture ....
   c product name ....

3 Choose the correct question:
   a What made you?
   b What did you make?
   c What you made?

4 You meet someone you think you know. What do you say?

5 Complete the question for this answer.
   Who ....?
   I worked for Nintendo.

6 Think of five questions you could ask someone about their family situation or personal interests.
   – Do …?
   – What …?
   – How often …?
   – Where …?
   – How many …?

1 Coca-Cola, IBM, and Microsoft. USA

03 Visiting companies
Travel

FOCUS ON WORDS 1: Company visits

1 Read this text, then work with a partner and answer the questions below.

This year for the first time, Texaco isn't flying MBA students to its headquarters for job interviews. Second interviews are being done by videoconference instead. Last month, Texaco managers saw and spoke with 120 MBA students on video at about twenty-five university and hotel locations around the world. The company saved twenty days of interviewing time and $300,000 in travel costs.

1 Why does Texaco conduct interviews by videoconference?
2 Would you like to be interviewed by videoconference? Why / Why not?
3 Why do many people prefer travelling to meetings rather than videoconferencing?

2 This is a list of reasons why people visit companies. Complete the gaps 1–5 with one of the verbs in the box.

give negotiate attend promote meet

1 to .... clients / colleagues
2 to .... a presentation / a training course
3 to .... meetings / job interviews
4 to .... products / services
5 to .... contracts / conditions

3 Are these things said by visitors (V) or people receiving visitors (R)?
1 Hello, I have an appointment to see Hans Geisler. ....
2 Do I need to sign in? ....
3 Would you like to have a look round before we start? ....
4 Did our receptionist give you your security pass? ....

4 Do you visit other companies? Do people visit your company? Why?

KEY WORDS
meet clients or colleagues *give a presentation* *negotiate a contract* *attend an interview* *promote products* *appointment* *sign in* *look round* *security pass*

FOCUS ON GRAMMAR: Countable and uncountable nouns

a

b

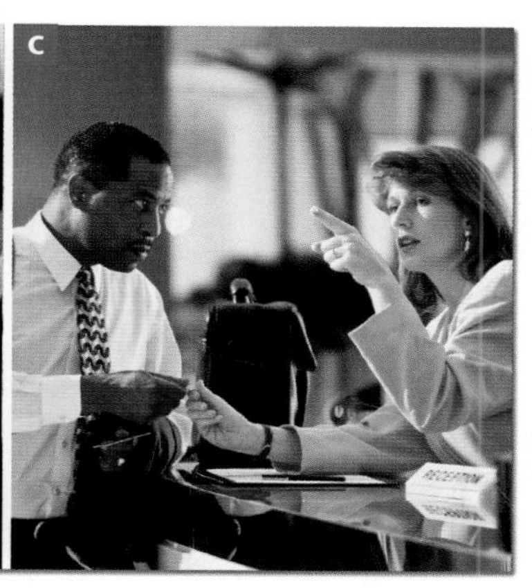
c

1 Match 1–6 to the photos above. There are two questions for each photo.

1 I need to change some (money). Are there any <u>banks</u> near here?
2 We want to go to Seville on Saturday. Is there a flight that leaves at about 7 a.m?
3 How much luggage have you got? You can only take one bag on the flight.
4 Do you have any information about hotels in the city centre?
5 How much time do I have before we board?
6 How many nights would you like to stay?

KEY GRAMMAR

Nouns in English can be *countable* or *uncountable*.
Countable nouns have a plural form (e.g. *bank* → *banks*).
Uncountable nouns have no plural form (e.g. *information* → ~~*informations*~~).
We use *how many?* with countable nouns, and *how much?* with uncountable nouns.
We use *is there?* with singular or uncountable nouns, and *are there*? with plural nouns.

For more on countable and uncountable nouns, see Language reference page 109.

2 <u>Underline</u> all the countable nouns and (circle) the uncountable nouns in **1** above.

3 Say if the words in the box are countable (C) or uncountable (U).

ticket	taxi	night	bank	research ....
equipment	minute	product	hour	business trip ....
travel	job	work	news	data ....

4 Complete these questions with *How much ...?*, *How many ...?*, *Is there ...?*, *Are there ...?* Then, work with a partner and ask and answer the questions.

1 .... hours a day do you work on your computer?
2 .... time do you spend packing for a holiday?
3 .... business trips do you make in a year?
4 .... employees from overseas in your company?
5 .... work do you have at the moment?
6 .... a good restaurant near your office?

5 (((3.1))) Complete these sentences with words from the box. Then, match the sentences to the questions in **1** on page 21, as in the example. Listen and check.

any some a much is are

a Yes, there .... one that leaves at 7.30. But .... there .... seats still free? Let me check. ...2...

b Well, I haven't got .... to check in – I've only got this small bag and my laptop. Have you got .... window seats? ....

c We don't have .... news at the moment. All we know is that there's .... delay on the incoming flight. I'm sure you'll have .... time to go shopping. ....

d Two, please. .... there .... rooms on the top floor with .... view of the city? I'd like to take .... photos. ....

e No, but I can do .... research for you. How .... are you prepared to pay per night? ....

f Well, there aren't .... banks within walking distance, but there's .... bureau de change in this hotel. ....

KEY GRAMMAR

In negative sentences and questions, we use *a* with singular nouns, and *any* with plural or uncountable nouns.

In positive sentences, we use *some* (not *any*) with plural or uncountable nouns.

For more on *some* and *any*, see Language reference page 109.

6 Work with a partner. Student A, turn to File 7 on page 86. Student B, turn to File 7 on page 94.

7 Put the parts of this email in the correct order 1–8.

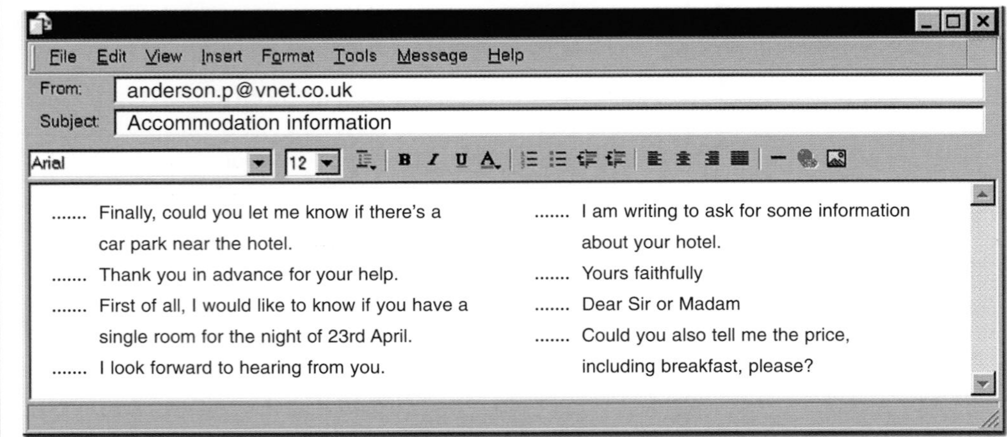

8 Now write a similar email to a hotel about their conference / meeting rooms.

- Rooms available for meetings?
- Cost of a conference room per day?
- Accommodation at the hotel?
- Cost of lunch?
- Train station nearby?

FOCUS ON WORDS 2: Travel

1 Work with a partner to complete the table below with words from the box. Words can go in more than one column, as in the example.

a timetable	a car park	single / double	one-way / return	a platform	to rent
to be delayed	to check in	an arrivals hall	a shuttle bus	to take off	to book
a motorway	to board	a petrol station	insurance	to land	to check out
departure	a gate	a safe	a terminal	a key	a fare
a connection	a bill	a seat-belt			

HOTEL	TRAIN	PLANE	CAR
	a timetable	*a timetable*	

2 Complete these notices with words from **1**. Sometimes you need to change the form of the word, for example: *to board* → *boarding*.

Guests are required to [1] .... before 11 a.m. Before vacating room, please remember to remove all valuables from [2] .... and to return [3] .... card to reception.

Flight	Destination	Time	Status
BA 12	Hong Kong	14.45	[4] .... until 16.30 Wait in lounge
UA 345	Seattle	15.30	Now [5] .... at [6] 26

Office closed 11 p.m.–5 a.m.
If returning a [7] .... car between these times, please leave in [8] .... and post [9] .... through letterbox.
N.B. Customers are advised to fill tank before leaving vehicle. There is a 24-hour [10] .... 500m from this office (see map below).

[11] .... to London from this station:
Single: £25
[12] ....: £32 (same day)
For information on departure times, please consult [13] .... in main concourse area.

3 3.2 Listen to five different announcements and conversations. Where would you hear them and what is happening?

4 Work with a partner. You are going to have four short conversations. Student A, turn to File 8 on page 87. Student B, turn to File 8 on page 95.

FOCUS ON EXPRESSIONS 1: Making offers

1 Look at the pictures. What do you think the people are saying?

2 3.3 Listen and match each conversation 1–4 to the pictures a–d in **1**.

3 3.3 Listen again and complete the questions in each picture. What was the visitor's response in each case?

4 Which of the four question forms in **1** (e.g. *Would you like to ...?*) are used to:
- ask if you can help another person?
- ask another person if they want to do something?

5 Work with a partner. Look at these situations and take it in turns to make and respond to offers. Use the expressions in **1**, as in the example.

A *Would you like a glass of water?*
B *Yes, please. That would be nice.*

1 Your visitor looks very thirsty.
2 Your visitor doesn't know anybody else in your office.
3 It's midday, and your visitor had breakfast at 6 o'clock this morning.
4 Your visitor doesn't have enough copies of a document for your meeting.
5 Your visitor doesn't have your latest brochure.
6 Your visitor loves opera. He's / She's free this evening.
7 Your visitor looks cold.

KEY EXPRESSIONS

Offering: *Would you like a / some ...?* *Yes, please. (That would be nice.)* *No thanks, (I'm fine).*
Shall I ...? / Would you like me to ...? *Yes, please, if you could. / That's very kind of you.* *No, thanks. That's OK.*
Inviting: *Would you like to ...?* *Yes, please. That's very nice of you.* *Thanks, but I'm afraid ...*

FOCUS ON EXPRESSIONS 2: Greeting visitors

1 You work for the Freebird Corporation in Lisbon. A customer is visiting you for the first time. Complete the welcoming phrases 1–7 with the words from the box.

Did you find ...?	Where ...?	Did you get ...?	Welcome ...
How long ...?	Did you have ...?	Would you like ...?	

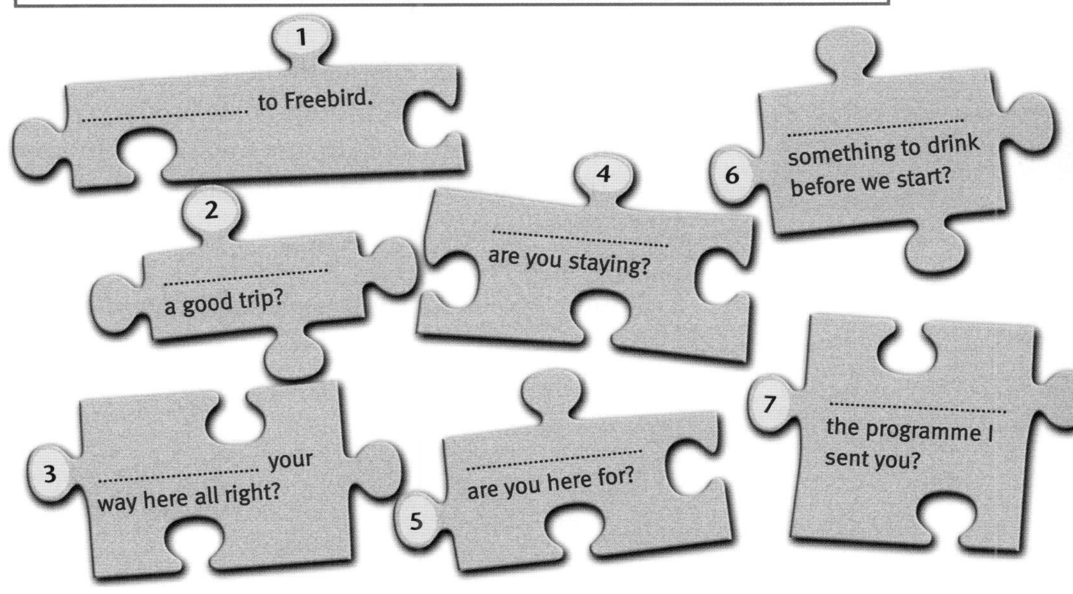

2 3.4 Now listen and check your answers. How does the visitor respond in each case? Practise the conversation with a partner.

3 3.5 We often ask follow-up questions to develop the conversation. Listen to a longer version of the conversation. Complete the follow-up questions below.

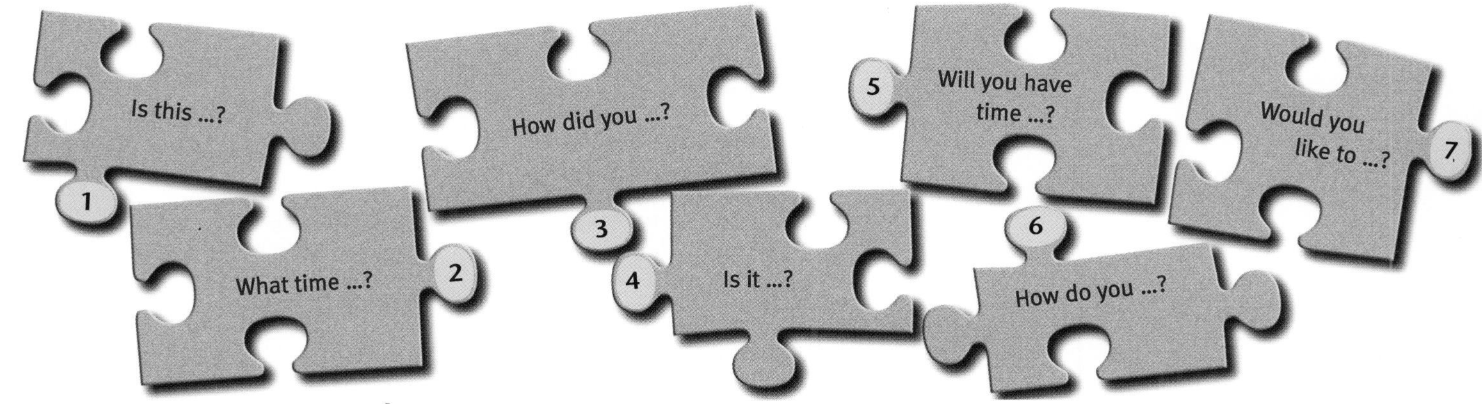

4 Work with a partner and role-play a conversation where a visitor is coming to **your** company. Use the questions in **1** and the follow-up questions in **3**. Then, change roles and role-play the conversation again.

KEY EXPRESSIONS

Greeting visitors: *Welcome to ... . Did you have a good trip? Did you find your way here all right? How long are you staying? Would you like something to drink?*

Responses: *Thanks very much. No problem. Yes, please. No, thanks. Yes, thanks. (It was fine.)*

FOCUS ON COMMUNICATION: Conversation game

Work with a partner and play this conversation game. You are going on a business trip. Have two-minute conversations for each place in the table below (travel agency, hotel reception, etc.), as in the example.

- Take it in turns to be the business traveller. The other person is the travel agent, airport employee, etc.
- The business traveller starts each conversation with the 'Conversation opener'.
- Use the question forms in the 'Questions' column to continue the conversation. Tick (✓) the 'Points' column every time you use one of the question forms. You can use the same forms as often as you like, but try to use them all before the end of the game. See the example below.
- The winner is the person who has the most points.

Travel agency:

Business traveller *I'd like some information about flights, please.* ***Are there*** *any flights to Moscow on a Sunday?* (1 point)

Travel agent *Yes, there are.* ***What time*** *do you want to leave?* (1 point)

PLACE	CONVERSATION OPENER	QUESTIONS	POINTS (✓)
TRAVEL AGENCY	I'd like some information about flights, please.	*What time …?* *Is there …?* *Where …?* *Are there …?* *How many …?* *How much …?* *How long …?* *Would you like to …?* *Would you like me to …?* *Shall I …?* *Can I …?* *Did you …?* *Do you have …?*	
AIRPORT INFORMATION DESK	Excuse me – I'm a little lost.		
CAR RENTAL DESK	Is it possible to rent a car without a reservation?		
HOTEL RECEPTION	I'm sorry, but I'm not happy with my room.		
CLIENT'S OFFICE	It's nice to see you again. I'm sorry I'm late.		
STATION TICKET OFFICE	I've just missed my train to Zurich.		
CONFERENCE INFORMATION DESK	I've just arrived. I'd like to register, please.		
CONFERENCE PARTY	Is this your first time at this conference?		
*Give yourself 1 point for each tick. Deduct 2 points for each question form you haven't used.		**Total points***	

FOCUS ON BUSINESS ISSUES: Doing business in a different culture

1 This text is about how we should greet and address Brazilians. Before you read it can you answer these questions? Then, read the text to see if you were right.

1 When do I shake hands?
2 Do I kiss women (or men) when I see them?

Brazilians are generally warm and friendly people. Shake hands every time you meet or say goodbye to a Brazilian, even if you met the same person earlier in the day. If you are a man, remember that Brazil is a Latin country: don't be surprised if Brazilian men stand very close to you, hold your hand or arm for a long time, or put their arm round your shoulders. This is a normal sign of friendship.

Shake hands with Brazilian women on a first meeting; after that they will probably kiss you on the cheek. If you are a woman on business, Brazilian men will shake hands on the first meeting, then perhaps kiss you after that.

2 A Brazilian businessman is talking about business culture in Brazil.

1 3.6 Listen and number these questions 1–4 in the order he talks about them.
- ❑ Can I talk business in a restaurant?
- ❑ Is it easy to conclude a deal?
- ❑ Do meetings and appointments usually start on time?
- ❑ Can I start talking business at the beginning of a meeting?

2 3.6 Listen again. What are the answers to the questions above?

3 Work with a partner. Ask and answer the questions in **1** and **2** for your country. Do you know the business culture of any other country?

END-OF-UNIT QUIZ

This is the end of Unit 3. Try this quick quiz to make sure you have understood everything.

1 Correct the two sentences that are wrong.
- a I'm afraid I don't have any informations about that.
- b Let me give you some help.
- c Is there any bank near here?
- d How much money do I need for a taxi to the station?
- e How many people are there on the bus?

2 You have a visitor to your company. Make three offers.
- a Would you like a …?
- b Would you like to …?
- c Would you like me to …?

3 Match the verbs in A to the nouns in B.

A	B
negotiate	presentations
promote	interviews
attend	contracts
give	products

4 What's the opposite of these phrases?
- a a one-way ticket ....
- b a single room ....
- c the plane takes off ....

04 Making decisions
Employment

FOCUS ON WORDS

1 Companies often give their staff more than a salary. They also give them benefits, such as a company car. Look at the list below. Do you get any of these benefits? Or any others? Which ones are most important to you?

1 Pension
2 Flexible working hours
3 Medical insurance
4 Maternity / paternity leave
5 Training
6 Paid holiday

2 Look at what people are saying in the cartoon and match a–f to a benefit in **1** above.

3 Two people are talking about their company benefits. One works for a US company and the other for a Swedish company.

1 4.1 Listen. Are they happy with all the benefits their companies offer?
2 4.1 Now listen again and complete this table.

BENEFITS	AMERICAN COMPANY	SWEDISH COMPANY
Pension	company pays 10% of salary	
Flexible working hours		10a.m. - 4p.m. + 15 hours
Maternity leave	8 weeks	
Company mobile phone		only for professional calls
Paid holiday	2 weeks	

4 Which company would you prefer to work for?

5 Work wth a partner. What do people think about when they look for a new job? Just money and benefits?

6 Here is some advice for people looking for a job from an Internet recruitment page. Complete the gaps with the words from the box.

vacancies training recruitment appraisal CV interview retire salary advertisements application benefits relocate

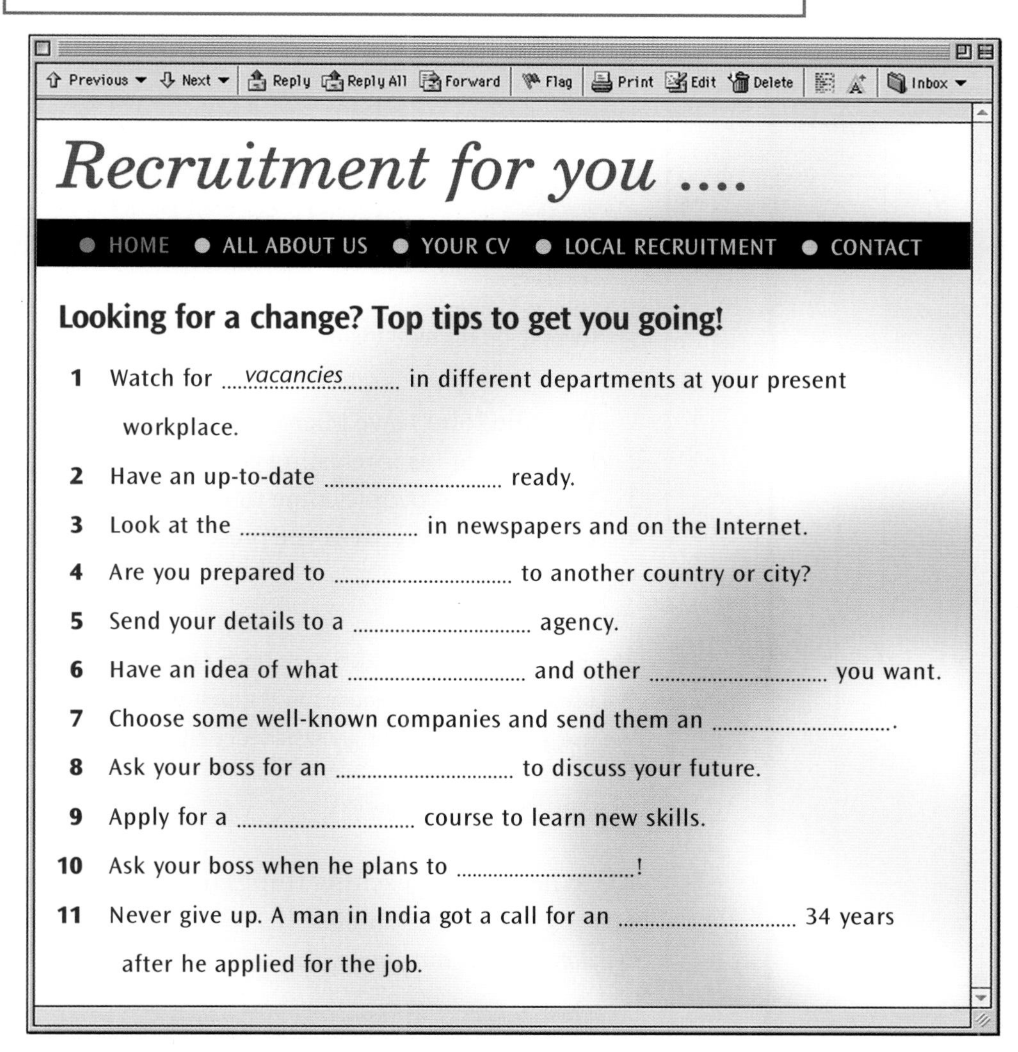

Recruitment for you ....

● HOME ● ALL ABOUT US ● YOUR CV ● LOCAL RECRUITMENT ● CONTACT

Looking for a change? Top tips to get you going!

1 Watch for *vacancies* in different departments at your present workplace.
2 Have an up-to-date .... ready.
3 Look at the .... in newspapers and on the Internet.
4 Are you prepared to .... to another country or city?
5 Send your details to a .... agency.
6 Have an idea of what .... and other .... you want.
7 Choose some well-known companies and send them an ....
8 Ask your boss for an .... to discuss your future.
9 Apply for a .... course to learn new skills.
10 Ask your boss when he plans to ....!
11 Never give up. A man in India got a call for an .... 34 years after he applied for the job.

7 Work with a partner. Tell them about when you got your present job. Talk about:

- how you found out about the job
- the interview
- why you liked the job.

Did you have interviews at other companies? Why did you choose this one?

KEY WORDS

application appraisal benefits CV (curriculum vitae) flexible interview maternity leave medical insurance paternity leave pension recruitment relocate retire salary training vacancies

FOCUS ON GRAMMAR: Present perfect and past simple

1 Read Part 1 of an article about people changing jobs. Answer the questions below.

John Chen *has bungee-jumped* from 120-foot-high bridges, has walked over red-hot coals and has parachuted from planes. But in his opinion the scariest thing he has ever done happened in 1999. He decided to leave his former employer Microsoft. Since then he has worked full-time for his own company, PlayTime.

PlayTime educates people in dealing with changes by giving them life-changing adventures, such as mountain climbing or swimming with dolphins. Over a third of the participants on his courses have changed jobs afterwards. His course is called The Journey and lasts one year.

bungee-jumping: jumping from a bridge attached to a piece of elastic
the scariest: the most frightening

1 Why did John leave Microsoft?
2 List some of his interesting activities.
3 What kind of people come to PlayTime?
4 Underline the verbs in the present perfect, as in the example.

KEY GRAMMAR

The *present perfect* is formed with *have / has* + the past participle of the main verb.
We use it to talk about actions in the past where the time *includes* the present.
We use *ever* to talk about an experience that happened at some time in your life.

For more on the present perfect, see Language reference page 116.

2 What scary or exciting things have you done in your life? Compare with a partner, as in the example.
I've done a parachute jump. I've visited India.

We can start a conversation using the present perfect.
A ***Have you been** to Sri Lanka?*
B *Yes, I **have**. / No, I **haven't**.*
If the answer is positive, we can continue with the past simple. For example:
*When **did** you **go**? How long **were** you there? Where **did** you **stay**?*, etc.

3 Work with a partner. Use the conversation starters in *italics* to develop conversations using your own ideas.
Have you heard about ... (the tornado in Florida)?
Have you seen ... (the new Spielberg movie)?
Have you tried ... (the new gym)?
Have you ever ... (been to the Far East)?

4 Now read Part 2 of the article. Answer the questions below.

A former colleague of John Chen's, Bruce Baker, spent four years at Microsoft before leaving in 1996. This scientist then spent four years training to be a priest and since December 2001 he has worked for the church. A third colleague, Peggy Fitzgerald, was a program manager for 10 years, from 1989 until 1999. She then quit, retrained and became a 'doula', or childbirth coach, in 2000.
So why did all these people leave well-paid corporate positions to take up more altruistic careers? 'The corporate world is a stepping stone,' Ms Fitzgerald observes. 'Learn skills while you're there and then go off and do something to give back.'

a childbirth coach: a person who gives advice to future mothers
altruistic: taking interest in other people more than yourself

1 How long was Bruce at Microsoft? When did he leave Microsoft?
2 How long did he study to be a priest? How long has he worked for the church?
3 Make two questions about Peggy using *How long ...?*

5 What do you think about these people? Have people left your company for similar reasons? Have you thought about it?

KEY GRAMMAR

We use the *present perfect* to talk about an action which started in the past but is not finished.
We use the *past simple* to describe an action which began and ended completely in the past.
We use *since* to describe the start of the action (e.g. *since 1997*) and *for* to describe the *length of time* of the action (e.g. *for three months*).

For more on the present perfect vs. the past simple, see Language reference page 116.

6 Complete the gaps with *for* or *since*.

1 .... years
2 .... May
3 .... three months
4 .... Tuesday
5 .... 6 o'clock
6 .... five hours

7 Work with a partner. Ask each other about your careers. Use these prompts.

- How long / present company?
- How long / current job?
- How many companies / work for?
- How long / continue your studies after the age of 18?
- Ever / do / completely different type of job? What?
- How long / study English at school?

FOCUS ON EXPRESSIONS: Making suggestions and arrangements

1 4.2 An HR manager, Anna Baxter, is preparing to interview three candidates for a new post. She is discussing her plans with her colleagues Marianne and George. Look at these suggestions. Which three suggestions are accepted?

1 What about interviewing them by phone?
2 I think we should invite them here on different days.
3 Why don't we invite them here on the same day?
4 We could also ask them to work together on a small project.
5 Let's get some coffee.

2 Look at the sentences in **1**. Underline the expressions used for making suggestions.

3 4.2 Listen again. How do they respond to suggestions 1–4 in **1**?

4 Work with a partner. Take it in turns to make suggestions in these situations. Use the expressions in **1**, as in the example.
Why don't we try the new Italian restaurant?

SITUATION	SUGGESTION
1 A colleague wants to have lunch.	the new Italian restaurant
2 You are launching a new product.	an email to all customers
3 A friend is unhappy with her salary.	meeting with her boss for an appraisal
4 You need a new supplier.	search on the Internet
5 A colleague looks unwell and tired.	leave early
6 Your boss needs help with phone calls in English.	take a language course
7 There are communication problems in your office.	a weekly meeting
8 A colleague wants to work abroad.	meeting with HR director to talk about vacancies

5 Now, for each situation in **4**, take it in turns to make a different suggestion and respond. Use the expressions you heard in **3**, as in the example.

A *Let's try the new Chinese restaurant for lunch.*
B *OK. Good idea. / No. I think I'd prefer ...*

6 Work with a partner. Write down three problems you have at work at the moment. Tell your partner. Listen to your partner's suggestions.

KEY EXPRESSIONS

Why don't I / you / we ...? *Good idea.* *How about ...?* *Fine.* *You / We could ...* *OK. Let's ...* *I'm not sure about that.* *Shall we ...?* *You should ...*

7 (((4.3))) Marianne needs to arrange the interviews. Look at her diary and listen to her first call to one candidate, Charles Lawson. Today is 3 June.

1 What dates are difficult or impossible for Charles?
2 What possible dates do they choose?
3 Do they arrange a time?

JUNE	Week 23	JUNE	Week 24
7 Monday		**14** Monday	
8 Tuesday		**15** Tuesday	
9 Wednesday		**16** Wednesday	
10 Thursday		**17** Thursday	
11 Friday		**18** Friday	

8 (((4.3))) Complete the gaps in the conversation with words from the box, then listen again and check your answers.

good	how about	available	time	shall	when	free	afraid	say	busy

M So, [1]................................ are you [2]................................?
C Which week are you talking about?
M Either next week – week twenty-three, or the week after – week twenty-four.
C Next week is difficult, so I'd prefer the week after.
M Right. That's the week beginning Monday the 14th. [3]................................ Tuesday the 15th?
C I'm free that day but the following day I'm in Madrid.
M Are you [4]................................ on the 17th and 18th?
C I'm [5]................................ I'm [6]................................ the morning of the 17th.
M OK, so [7]................................ we [8]................................ the afternoon of the 17th and then all day on the 18th?
C That would be fine. What [9]................................ is [10]................................ for you?

9 Work with a partner. Take it in turns to be Marianne and arrange times with the other candidates. Use the diary above. Remember the dates you have already agreed with Charles Lawson.

1 Student A you are Marianne. Call Student B, Emilie Thomas, to find two days that she is free. Student B, turn to File 9 on page 95.
2 Student B now you are Marianne. Call Student A, Philip Johnson, to find two days that he is free. Student A, turn to File 9 on page 87.

KEY EXPRESSIONS

When are you free?   Are you available on / at … ?   How / What about …?   How does … suit you?
What time is good for you?   Shall we say … ?   So that's (time) on (day / date).

FOCUS ON COMMUNICATION

1 Write a job advertisement for your ideal job. Complete the box below.

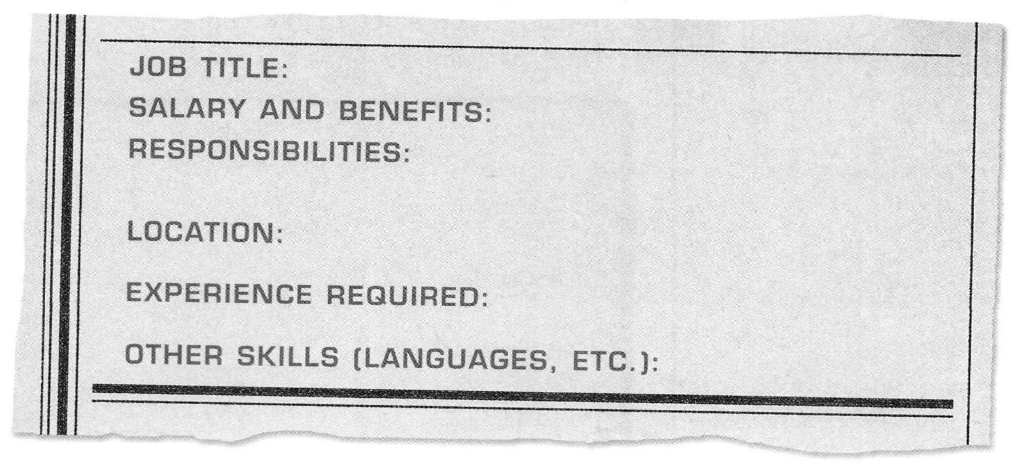

JOB TITLE:
SALARY AND BENEFITS:
RESPONSIBILITIES:
LOCATION:
EXPERIENCE REQUIRED:
OTHER SKILLS (LANGUAGES, ETC.):

2 You want to apply for this job. Make a list of questions you think an interviewer would ask you.
What experience do you have of this type of work?
How long have you worked for your present company?
What questions would you ask? Make a list.
Could you tell me about the salary?

3 Work with a partner. Exchange your job advertisements and lists of questions. Interview your partner for his / her ideal job. Then, change roles. Your partner interviews you for your ideal job.

4 Now complete this email to confirm the arrangements for a second interview. Use the words in the box below.

do not hesitate to email me or phone me	on Tuesday June 11th
would like to show you around at 4.30	our phone conversation
look forward to seeing you again	will reimburse you as agreed
have arranged overnight accommodation for you	confirm the following details

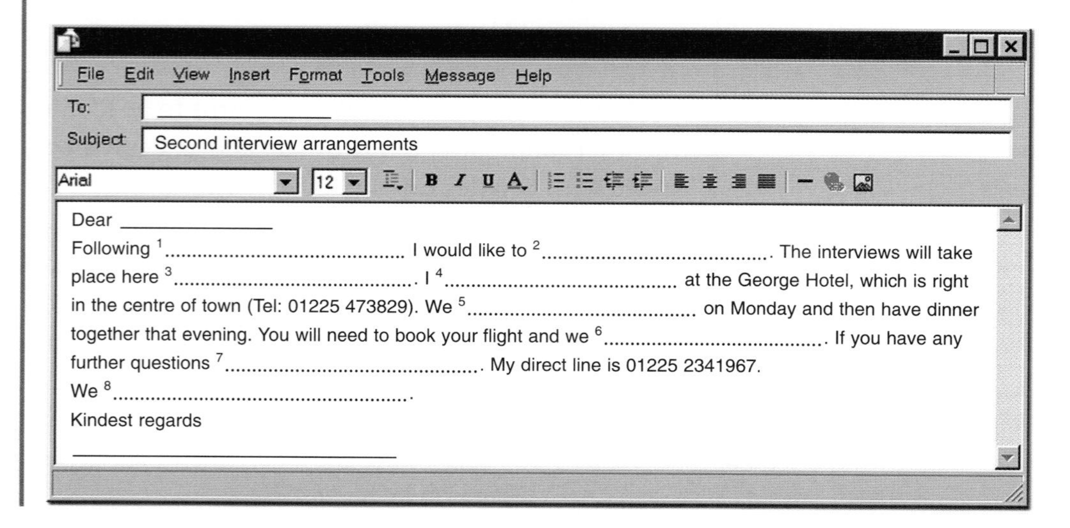

File Edit View Insert Format Tools Message Help
To: ______
Subject: Second interview arrangements

Dear ______
Following [1].................... I would like to [2].................... The interviews will take place here [3].................... I [4].................... at the George Hotel, which is right in the centre of town (Tel: 01225 473829). We [5].................... on Monday and then have dinner together that evening. You will need to book your flight and we [6].................... If you have any further questions [7].................... My direct line is 01225 2341967.
We [8]....................
Kindest regards
______

WORDS
Job benefits and recruitment

GRAMMAR
Present perfect and past simple

EXPRESSIONS
Making suggestions and arrangements

COMMUNICATION
An interview
Email to confirm arrangements

BUSINESS ISSUES
Choosing the right job

END-OF-UNIT QUIZ

FOCUS ON BUSINESS ISSUES: Choosing the right job

1 Work with a partner. Look at the picture. Which job would you most like to do? And least like to do? Why? Why do people change jobs?

2 Here are five reasons for changing jobs. What advice would you give these people?

1 I work for the family firm. I'd like to try the outside world.
2 My job is boring.
3 I want to do something to help the world.
4 I love my hobby. I want a job where I can use this interest.
5 I left school when I was very young. I'm not really qualified to do anything.

3 4.4 Three people telephone a radio programme to ask for career advice. Listen and for each caller write down their problem from the list in 2.

1 Caller 1 .... 2 Caller 2 .... 3 Caller 3 ....

4 4.4 Listen again and complete the advice each caller receives.

1 Caller 1: You could get .... a sailing instructor.
2 Caller 2: Go to .... and get some qualifications.
3 Caller 3: Try the outside world for a couple of years but make sure the family business will .... back if you want to.

5 Tell your partner how and why you chose your career.

END-OF-UNIT QUIZ

This is the end of Unit 4. Try this quick quiz to check you have understood everything.

1 If we ask someone: *How long were you married?*, is the person still married?
2 If I say: *I've been to Brazil*, what is the next logical question?
3 Complete with *for* or *since*.
   a I've worked here .... 1991.
   b She's worked here .... five years.
4 What is the word for the group of best candidates for a job? Is it: *toplist*, *shortlist*, *shortline?*
5 How many company benefits can you think of?
6 Suggest a destination to someone for a weekend away.
7 You want to meet someone the day after tomorrow at 5.00 p.m. Ask them.
8 What can you say to change the time of a meeting?

05 Comparing information
Customer satisfaction

FOCUS ON WORDS

1 Look at the pictures. What problems are the people having?

2 5.1 A lot of people experience poor customer service. Listen to five people talking about their bad experiences and answer these questions.

1 What was the problem with the book? What did he do?
2 Why did she need a taxi? What happened?
3 Why did she ask for a replacement buggy? How long did it take?
4 Why did he call after-sales support? Was the employee helpful?
5 Why does she want to change supermarket?

3 Now match suggestions a–e to the problems 1–5 in **2** to say how the businesses can improve their customer service.

a They should give refunds if they want to get repeat business. ....
b They should improve the quality of their goods and their after-sales service. ....
c They should give regular customers loyalty cards. ....
d They should make sure that employees at their call centre are always polite. ....
e They should make their service more reliable. ....

4 5.2 Now listen to these conversations and check your answers.

5 Complete these sentences with words in the box.

loyal	satisfied	dissatisfied	reliable	unreliable

1 My bus always arrives on time – it is a .... service.
2 I always shop at the same supermarket – I am a very .... customer.
3 Their after-sales service is excellent – I am a very .... customer.
4 I am very .... with their service – they always deliver things late.
5 They never call me back when they say they will – they are very ....

6 Have you stopped using a company's products or services because of a bad experience? Work with a partner and tell them what happened.

7 Match the verbs in A to the nouns in B.

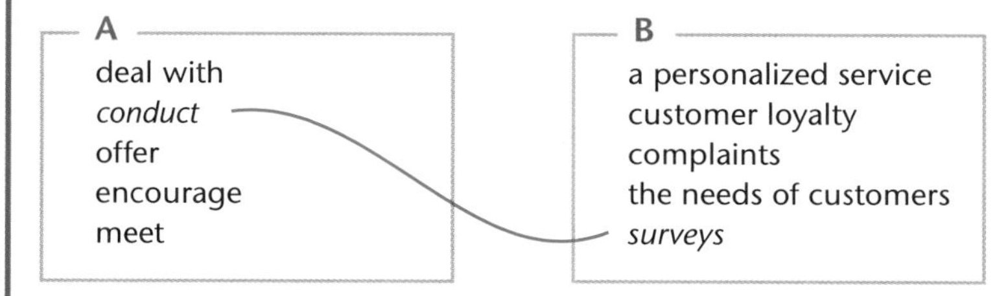

A	B
deal with	a personalized service
conduct	customer loyalty
offer	complaints
encourage	the needs of customers
meet	*surveys*

8 A company is answering frequently asked questions about its services. Study the answers, and choose expressions from **7** to complete the questions. What type of company is it?

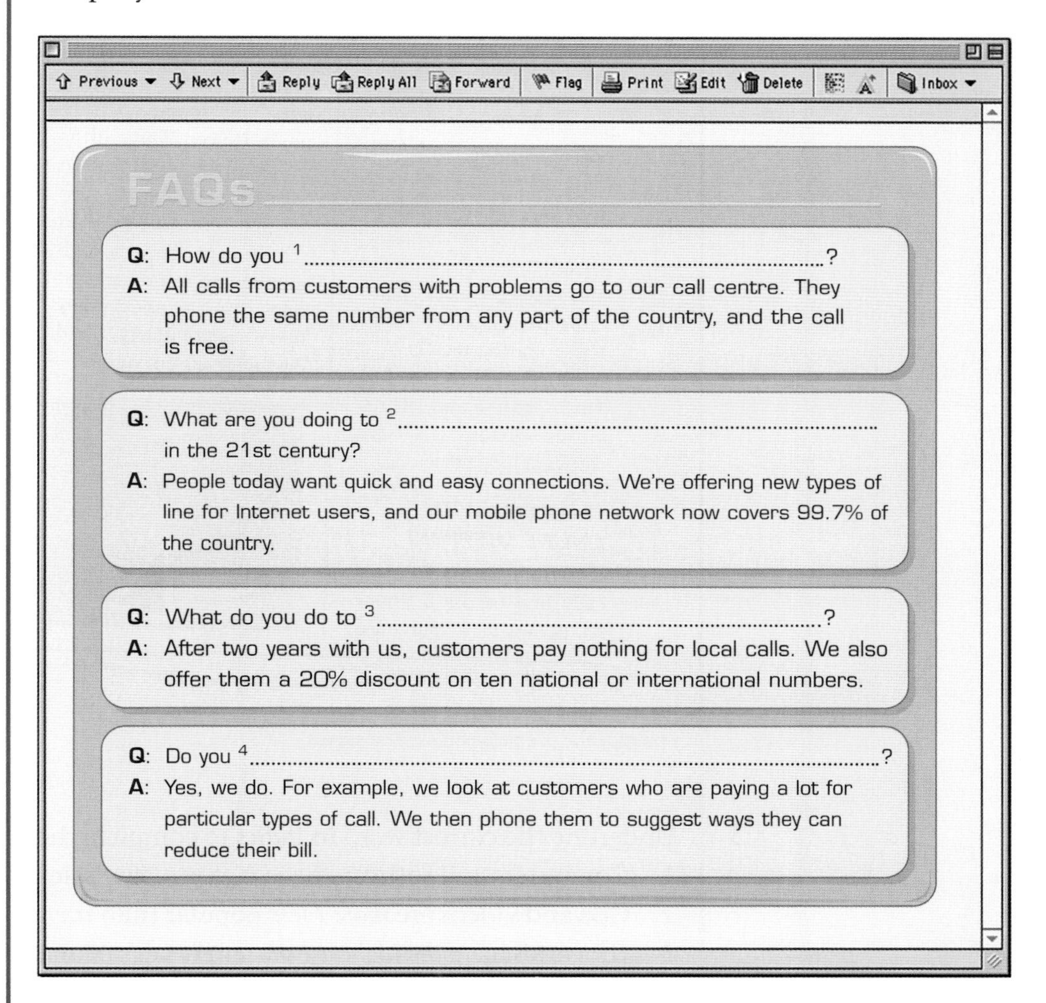

FAQs

Q: How do you [1] ....?
A: All calls from customers with problems go to our call centre. They phone the same number from any part of the country, and the call is free.

Q: What are you doing to [2] .... in the 21st century?
A: People today want quick and easy connections. We're offering new types of line for Internet users, and our mobile phone network now covers 99.7% of the country.

Q: What do you do to [3] ....?
A: After two years with us, customers pay nothing for local calls. We also offer them a 20% discount on ten national or international numbers.

Q: Do you [4] ....?
A: Yes, we do. For example, we look at customers who are paying a lot for particular types of call. We then phone them to suggest ways they can reduce their bill.

9 Work with a partner. How many of the questions in **8** can you answer for:
- the company you work for?
- your own phone company (for mobile or fixed-line services)?

KEY WORDS

after-sales support *call centres* *dissatisfied* *loyalty cards* *quality* *refunds* *reliable* *repeat business* *satisfied* *unreliable*

WORDS
Customer service
GRAMMAR
Comparatives and superlatives
More / less / fewer
EXPRESSIONS
Asking for and giving opinions
Stressing words for emphasis
COMMUNICATION
Exchanging personal views
Email of recommendation
BUSINESS ISSUES
Customer service experiences
END-OF-UNIT QUIZ

FOCUS ON GRAMMAR: Comparatives and superlatives

1 Work with a partner and answer these questions.

1 What do you think is the main reason why people *don't* buy goods on the Internet?
2 What do you think are the best-selling products on the Internet?

2 Now read the text below quickly and find the answers to the questions in **1**. Is there anything that surprises you?

Customer service and the Internet

TO BUY OR NOT TO BUY ONLINE?

A lot of people think that Internet security is the main reason for not buying online. In fact, what stops most people from buying immediately is the desire to compare prices with other web-sites and problems with Internet connections. These are the results of a survey conducted by *The Times* with Kana, which makes customer service software for business.

PROBLEMS WITH ONLINE SHOPPING

59% of shoppers said they had to use a phone to complete a purchase. Almost half said that the Internet site didn't have their personal details every time they revisited a site. This made ordering much slower. Three-fifths of shoppers said that in the future they would stop buying online after a bad service experience. A high number of respondents – one third – said they had 'particularly bad customer service online'.

THE TOP SITES

The most popular online products were books, CDs, and videos (77%), followed by software and computers (56%). Travel came third, with a 47% vote. Grocery sales were at the bottom, with a 20% vote, probably because supermarkets don't offer a very good delivery service at the moment.

grocery: food products
respondents: people who answer a survey

3 Underline the correct word in *italics* to complete these statements about the text.

1 Computers and software have *higher / lower* sales than groceries.
2 CDs and videos are *more / less* popular than travel.
3 Groceries have *the highest / the lowest* sales of all the products.
4 The two *least / most* important reasons for not buying online were the desire to compare prices and connection problems.
5 CDs and videos are the *best / worst*-selling products online.
6 Nearly 50% of people had to spend *less / more* time giving their personal details again.
7 *Fewer / More* than 50% of customers had to use a phone to complete an order.

KEY GRAMMAR

The comparative form of adjectives like *high* is *higher* and the superlative form is *the highest*.
The comparative form of longer adjectives like *important* is *more important* and the superlative form is *the most important*.
The superlative form of *good* is *the best* and *bad* is *the worst*.
The opposite of *the most* is *the least*.
With uncountable nouns like *time*, we use *more* and *less*.
With plural countable nouns like *customers*, we use *more* and *fewer*.

For more on comparatives, superlatives and *more / less / fewer*, see Language reference page 106.

4 Work with a partner. Student A, turn to File 10 on page 88. Student B, turn to File 10 on page 96.

5 Complete the text with an appropriate form of the adjective in brackets. Where there is more than one possibility, decide which word is better, for example:

1 *more loyal* or *less loyal*?
2 *most popular* or *least popular*?

Loyalty: People were (loyal) [1] more loyal to sites which were personalized and easy to use. The (popular) [2] least popular of all the sites were those with no customer service telephone number.
Female shoppers: For women, security was (important) [3] .... than anything else when buying online. They were slightly (interested) [4] .... in price than men. Women also wanted (good) [5] .... human contact through telephone helplines, and (quick) [6] .... registration procedures.
Silver surfers: The (old) [7] .... age groups were (happy) [8] .... to buy from sites operated by the most well-known shops, and from those which had the (short) [9] .... registration procedures.
Internet access: The (popular) [10] .... ISPs in the UK were Freeserve, AOL, and BTInternet.

registration procedures: typing your name, personal details, etc.
silver surfers: people more than 60 years old who use the Internet
ISPs: Internet service providers

6 5.3 Now listen and compare your answers.

7 Where do you prefer to do your food shopping – in a small local shop, a big supermarket, or online? Compare the three types of shopping and explain your opinions to a partner, as in the example. Think about the things below.

- distance
- time / speed
- number of people
- prices
- security
- choice
- personal attention

Local shops are usually nearer your home than supermarkets.
Online shopping probably takes the least time / is probably the quickest.

FOCUS ON EXPRESSIONS: Asking for and giving opinions

1 The words in the box are often used in meetings for asking for or giving opinions. How many expressions do you know using these words?

think agree point feel

2 Each person around this table is using one of the words in **1** to ask for and give opinions. Which word are they using?

3 Which expressions in **2** are used to:

1 ask for an opinion?
2 give an opinion?
3 agree?
4 disagree?

4 Pronunciation: stressing words for emphasis. In meetings, we often stress particular words to give more emphasis to our opinions.

1 5.4 Listen to these three short dialogues and underline the words that are stressed, as in the example. Which word is stressed the most?

1

A I think we should do it now. What do you think?
B I think so too. What about you, Chris?
C I don't agree. I feel we should wait.

2

D I think it's too late to do anything now.
E Yes, I agree. How do you feel about this, Frances?
F Well, I take your point, but I don't think time is a problem.

3

G It's a little expensive, Helen. Don't you agree?
H No, I don't think so. The cost is lower than last time.
I Yes, that's a good point.

2 When you have finished, practise the dialogue with a partner or partners.

5 What do you think of the ideas below? Work with a partner or in groups of three and exchange opinions, as in **4**.

1 Staff should always be polite to customers.
2 The best customers should get the best service.
3 The customer is always right.
4 Customer complaints are good for a company.
5 Customers don't always tell the truth in questionnaires.

6 Do you know how to talk about meetings? Match the words and phrases in the box to the definitions 1–6.

item	proposal	agenda	minutes	action points	AOB

1 the report of what happened in a meeting ....
2 a list of points to be discussed ....
3 one point to be discussed ....
4 decisions taken at a meeting about what to do ....
5 any other business (various other points for discussion) ....
6 an idea or suggestion ....

7 You work for Pan-European Oil, PEO, which has petrol stations in your country / countries. PEO wants to improve customer service in petrol stations. You are going to have a meeting to discuss different ideas on this subject.
Look at the agenda for your meeting. How many items are there on the agenda? How many proposals are there?

PEO Agenda for management meeting 14 March

1 Minutes of last meeting
2 Ideas for improving customer service:
 a introduce new loyalty card: customers get 1 free litre of petrol for every 200 litres bought
 b improve quality of food in petrol station cafés
 c employ new staff to operate petrol pumps for customers
 d offer half-price car wash when customers buy 40 litres of petrol
3 AOB

8 Work with a partner or in groups of three or four. Discuss the four proposals in **7** for improving customer service, and decide which one to accept. Student A, turn to File 11 on page 88. Student B, turn to File 12 on page 97. In groups of three, Student C, turn to File 1 on page 101. In groups of 4, Student D, turn to File 3 on page 102.

KEY EXPRESSIONS

Giving opinions: *I think / don't think … I feel / don't feel … We / they should … I don't think we / they should …*
Asking for opinions: *Do you agree? Don't you agree? What do you think? How do you feel about that?*
Agreeing and disagreeing: *I agree with you. I think so too. That's a good point. I don't agree. I don't think so. I take your point, but …*

FOCUS ON COMMUNICATION

1 When you have a problem as a customer, what makes the difference between good and bad customer service?

1 Think of a shop or other supplier you use often, e.g. a telephone or computer company, an electrical or hi-fi shop. How good is their customer service? Describe your 'personal experience' by completing the questionnaire below. Give each point a score from 0 to 4, as indicated.

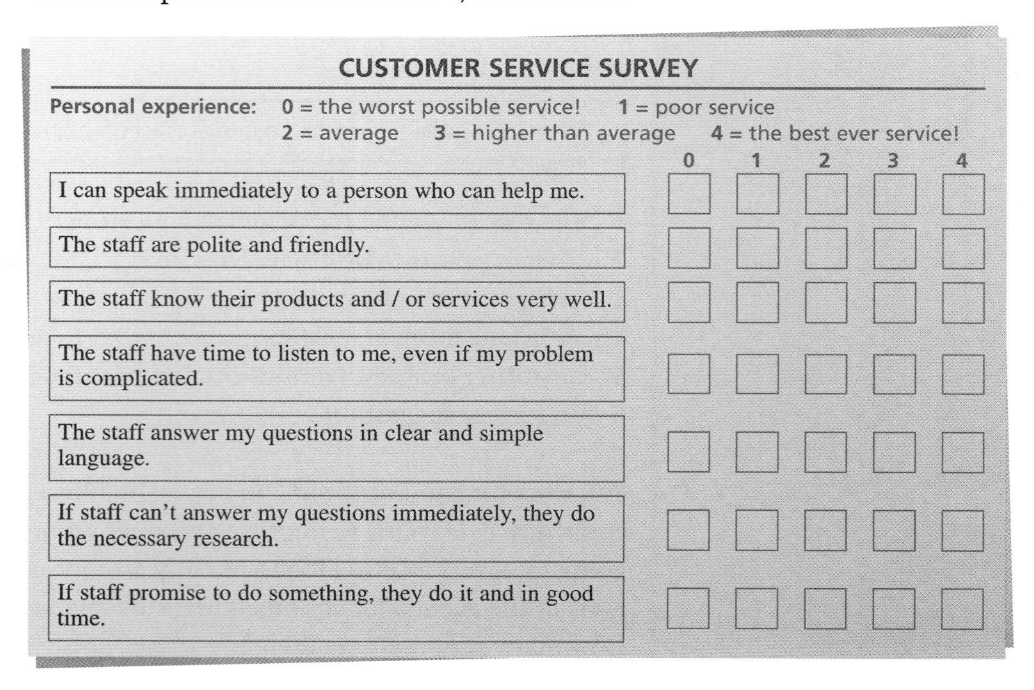

CUSTOMER SERVICE SURVEY

Personal experience: 0 = the worst possible service! 1 = poor service 2 = average 3 = higher than average 4 = the best ever service!

	0	1	2	3	4
I can speak immediately to a person who can help me.					
The staff are polite and friendly.					
The staff know their products and / or services very well.					
The staff have time to listen to me, even if my problem is complicated.					
The staff answer my questions in clear and simple language.					
If staff can't answer my questions immediately, they do the necessary research.					
If staff promise to do something, they do it and in good time.					

2 Now compare your questionnaire with a partner, and explain the answers you gave. If you and your partner answered for the same company, who has the more positive experience? If you answered for two different companies, which one seems to have the better customer service and why?

2 Read this email. Which hotel does the writer recommend?

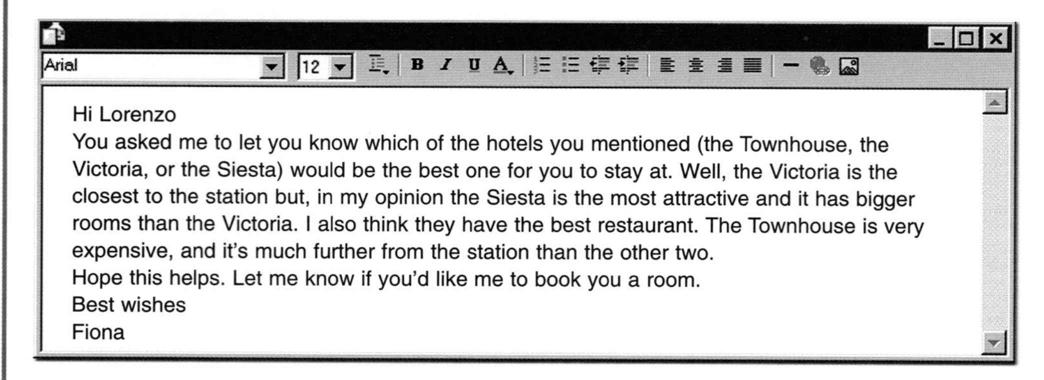

Hi Lorenzo
You asked me to let you know which of the hotels you mentioned (the Townhouse, the Victoria, or the Siesta) would be the best one for you to stay at. Well, the Victoria is the closest to the station but, in my opinion the Siesta is the most attractive and it has bigger rooms than the Victoria. I also think they have the best restaurant. The Townhouse is very expensive, and it's much further from the station than the other two.
Hope this helps. Let me know if you'd like me to book you a room.
Best wishes
Fiona

3 A customer has asked you about three restaurants in your town because they want to have a business lunch at one of them. Think of three restaurants in your town and write an email like the one in **2** saying what you think of them and recommending one.

WORDS
Customer service
GRAMMAR
Comparatives and superlatives
More / less / fewer
EXPRESSIONS
Asking for and giving opinions
Stressing words for emphasis
COMMUNICATION
Exchanging personal views
Email of recommendation
BUSINESS ISSUES
Customer service experiences
END-OF-UNIT QUIZ

FOCUS ON BUSINESS ISSUES: Customer service experiences

1 We say *Wow!* when we are impressed. What do you think *to wow your customers* means?

The most important thing in customer service is knowing how to wow your customers!

2 Mary Sandro is a professional trainer. The cartoon above shows a situation where she received very good service. What do you think happened?

3 5.5 Now listen to Mary and answer these questions.

1. What time of day did Mary arrive at the hotel?
2. What was Mary's problem?
3. How did the hotel receptionist 'wow' Mary Sandro?

4 Discuss the following questions in groups.

1. Do you agree with the caption in the cartoon?
2. What can / does your company do to 'wow' its customers?

5 Do you have a story about excellent customer service? What happened?

END-OF-UNIT QUIZ

This is the end of Unit 5. Try this quick quiz to make sure you have understood everything.

1 Match the words in A and B to make four two-word expressions.

A	online	customer	repeat	call
B	shopping	centre	loyalty	business

2 Correct the mistake in each of these sentences:

- a How do you think about this?
- b Are you agree with me?
- c I think we shouldn't to do it – it's too expensive.
- d I agree your point, but we have no other solution.

3 What is the opposite of these sentences?

a	Online shopping is	cheaper more difficult slower	than I thought.
b	He's our	newest best most loyal	customer.

06 Dealing with problems
Orders

FOCUS ON WORDS

1 Work with a partner.

1 Think of common problems people can have with orders for goods, for example: goods are damaged when you receive them.
2 What sort of goods have you ordered for home? And for work?
3 How did you order them? Was it easy?
4 Have you had any of the problems you discussed in 1? What happened?

2 Read the text and match the words in *italics* to these definitions.

1 a request to buy goods ....
2 to transport goods to a customer ....
3 to buy ....
4 to say how much something will cost ....
5 to deal with, e.g. an order ....
6 goods which are being transported ....
7 to follow the progress of an order online ....

UPS and MisterArt.com

MisterArt.com is the world's largest online discount art supply store. Customers can *purchase* goods 24 hours a day, 7 days a week and choose from more than 40,000 products. MisterArt.com needs to *deliver* goods quickly and also give customers great choice, great prices and great customer service.

UPS, the world's largest express delivery company, allows MisterArt.com to *process* the customer's *order* faster. With UPS OnLine® Tools on its web site, MisterArt.com can *quote* its customers prices for a wide choice of delivery options. Customers can return to the MisterArt.com site any time they like to *track* their *shipments*, because MisterArt.com uses the UPS order tracking system.

3

Complete this table.

VERB	NOUN
order	[1] ....
[2]	delivery
ship	[3] ....
[4]	purchase
[5]	quotation
[6]	process
pay	payment
track	×

4

(((6.1))) The flow chart below shows a typical order process. Choose words from the table in **3** to complete the chart. Then listen to a supplier describing the process and check your answers.

The customer ...	The supplier ...	The customer ...	The supplier ...
makes an enquiry about the supplier's products and the price.	provides information and a [1] .... for the product or service.	places an [2] .... with the supplier by phone, fax, or email.	begins to [3] .... the order: – checks that the product is in stock – confirms the order with the customer – gives the customer a date for [4] .... of the goods.

The customer ...	The supplier ...	The customer ...
[7] .... the invoice.	delivers the [6] .... to the customer.	[5] .... the progress of the order online.

5

What was the last thing you ordered? Tell your partner about the process, as in the example.

I placed an order for a new keyboard last week. I ordered it on the Internet. The company sent me an email to confirm my order and to give me a delivery date ...

6

You've ordered a book online to give to a friend for their birthday. Use the ideas in the box to say what you would do in the situations below.

> cancel your order   send the book back   track your order   ask for a refund
> change your order   check what they have in stock   make a complaint

1. You get a message to say that they are out of stock.
2. You receive the wrong book.
3. They charge you for the wrong amount.
4. The book hasn't arrived – it's your friend's birthday in three days' time.
5. The book is delivered the day after your friend's birthday.

KEY WORDS

check confirm deliver delivery enquire enquiry in stock out of stock invoice order process purchase quote quotation shipment track

FOCUS ON GRAMMAR 1: *Will* and *going to*

1 6.2 Listen to a customer phoning a supplier about a delivery and complete the information on the message pad below.

Client: [1] .... Engineering
Order Number: [2] ....
Delivery date: [3] ....
Delivery time: [4] ....
Action: Please change delivery time to [5] .... (same day)

2 6.2 Listen again to the second half of the conversation and complete these sentences.

1 No problem. .... just .... the delivery details.
2 Yes, they .... between ten and eleven.

KEY GRAMMAR

We use *going to* + main verb to talk about something that's already arranged.
We use *will* + main verb to make a decision at the moment of speaking.

For more on *will* and *going to*, see Language reference page 110.

3 Match the sentences 1–5 to the responses a–e. Then put the verb in brackets into an appropriate form, using *will* or *going to*.

1 Have you got any plans for this weekend? ....
2 Can we talk about this again next week? ....
3 I'm afraid I can't answer your question. ....
4 Have you decided what to do about the new sales post? ....
5 I'm sorry, but I can't be there for a meeting in the morning. ....

a Yes, I (give) .... you a call.
b Yes, we (advertise) .... in the national newspapers.
c Then we (change) .... the time to 2 p.m.
d That's OK. I (ask) .... somebody else.
e I (stay) .... with some friends who have a house by the sea.

4 Work with a partner. Student A, turn to File 12 on page 89. Student B, turn to File 11 on page 96.

FOCUS ON EXPRESSIONS: Giving bad news and saying sorry

1 These three people are all trying to resolve problems with customers or suppliers. What do you think the problems are?

2 6.3 Listen and match each conversation to the cartoons in **1**. Which two people are customers, and which is a supplier?

1 Conversation 1 .... 2 Conversation 2 .... 3 Conversation 3 ....

3 6.3 Listen again and complete these sentences which appear in the three conversations.

1 .... we don't have them in stock at the moment.
2 Oh, ... about that.
3 .... for the mistake.
4 .... we can't find your invoice.

4 Which of the expressions you wrote in **3** are used to:

– give bad news? – say sorry?

5 Match these possible responses to the sentences in **3** above.

Don't worry. That's OK. Oh dear. That's a pity.

6 Work with a partner. Student A, turn to File 13 on page 89. Student B, turn to File 13 on page 97.

7 6.3 Listen to the conversations in **2** again. Listen to the solutions that are offered and the responses. Complete these sentences.

1 Yes, of course. .... give you a call.
2 .... send you the rest today?
3 .... If you could.
4 No, ...

KEY EXPRESSIONS

Giving bad news and responding: *I'm afraid ... I'm (very) sorry, but ... That's a pity. Oh dear! / Oh no!*

Saying sorry and responding: *I'm (very) sorry about that. I do apologize for that / for our mistake. Don't worry.*

8 A supplier has to give bad news to his / her customers, then offer a solution. Match sentences 1–6 with solutions a–f. Then make sentences, as in the example.
I'm sorry, but I'm afraid your delivery will be a day or two late. Shall I call again when I know the exact delivery time?

BAD NEWS

1 Delivery will be a day or two late.
2 You can't give price information on the phone.
3 The online ordering service isn't working.
4 Your transporter's drivers are on strike.
5 You don't have the products in stock.
6 Nobody is in the Sales Department today.

SOLUTIONS

a call again when you have them
b call again when you know the exact delivery time
c note the details of the enquiry
d take the order by phone
e ship the products by rail
f send a quotation by fax

9 Take it in turns to be the supplier and customer, and develop the conversations in **8**. Use the expressions you wrote in **3** and **7**, as in the example.

Supplier *I'm afraid delivery will be a day or two late.*
Customer *Oh dear. / Well, that's a pity.*
Supplier *Yes, I do apologize for the delay. Shall I call you again when I have the exact delivery time?*
Customer *Yes, please, if you could. / No, that's OK. I think I'll cancel the order.*

10 Read this reply to a complaint. What do you think the letter of complaint said?

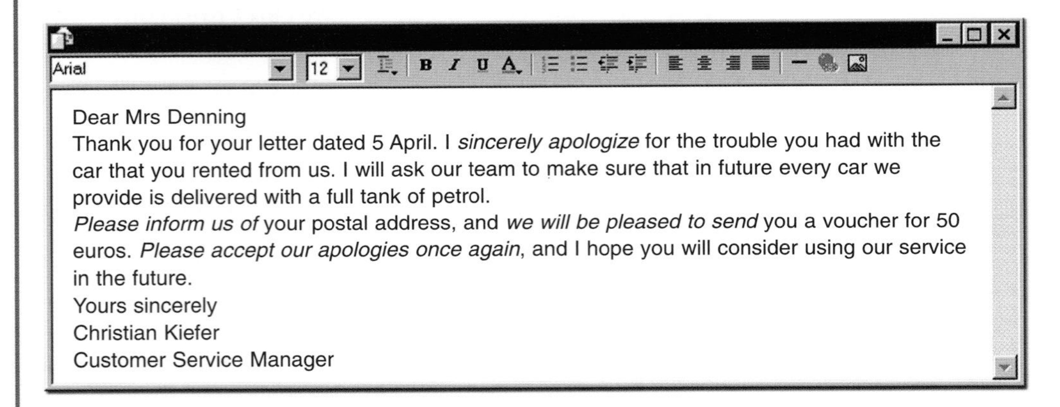

Dear Mrs Denning
Thank you for your letter dated 5 April. I *sincerely apologize* for the trouble you had with the car that you rented from us. I will ask our team to make sure that in future every car we provide is delivered with a full tank of petrol.
Please inform us of your postal address, and *we will be pleased to send* you a voucher for 50 euros. *Please accept our apologies once again*, and I hope you will consider using our service in the future.
Yours sincerely
Christian Kiefer
Customer Service Manager

11 Look at the words in *italics*. What should we say if we *speak* to the person?

12 Choose one of these situations and write a complaint to your partner. Your partner should then respond. Use the examples in **10** and on page 47 to help you.

1 Your train was cancelled so you missed your meeting.
2 You attended a very badly-organized training course.
3 A hotel receptionist was very rude to you.

KEY EXPRESSIONS

Offering action and responding: *I'll …* *No, that's OK.* *Shall I …?* *That's a pity.* *That's annoying.* *Yes, please, if you could.* *Oh dear.*

FOCUS ON GRAMMAR 2: *Will* and *going to*

1 Read about these four people. What predictions can you make?

1 *Mario's going to look for a new job. He's going to ...*

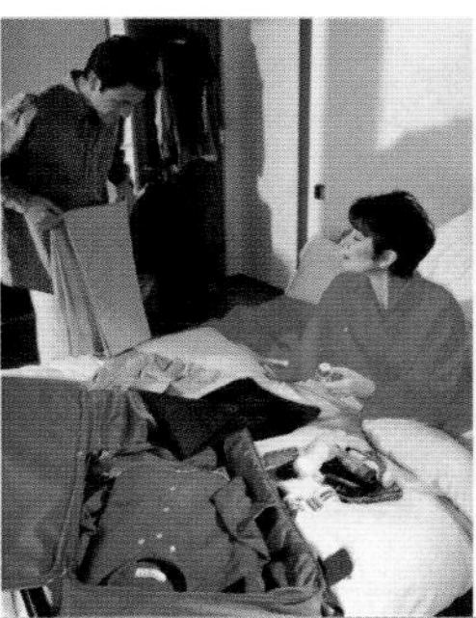

1 Mario works for a computer company. He's preparing a new version of his CV.
2 John and Chloe are packing. They are making sure they have everything they need.
3 Agnetha is calling a friend during working hours. She doesn't know her boss is listening outside.
4 Bernard is stuck in traffic. He has an important meeting in ten minutes.

2 Think about your office and make some predictions about how it will be different in twenty years' time, as in the example.

There won't be fax machines because we will send everything by email.

KEY GRAMMAR

We use *be going to* if we can see that something is about to happen.
We use *will* to say what we think or believe about the future.

For more on *will* and *going to*, see Language reference page 110.

3 Complete the sentences with *be / not be going to* or *will / won't*.

1 I hope it .... be a nice day tomorrow.
2 Look at these figures – you can see it .... be a hard year for us.
3 There is a lot of work here – I .... be able to finish it today.
4 He is raising his hand – he .... ask a question.
5 Don't ask him. He .... know the answer.
6 You look tired – I think you .... fall asleep!

4 Do you agree with these opinions? Discuss your answers with a partner.

1 People are going to use the Internet less because of viruses.
2 In ten years' time, non-voters will probably outnumber voters in presidential and national elections.
3 Because of global warming, water is going to become one of the most expensive resources in the world.
4 People will be less interested in money than quality of life.

FOCUS ON COMMUNICATION

1 Look at the cartoons. How would you respond to the different questions and comments?

2 Look at the table below.

1 Match responses 1–7 with sentences a–g above.

RESPONSES	CONVERSATION IDEAS
1 I'm sure children will love it.	– older people buy? where / sell? how many / sell?
2 I'll put you through to Accounts.	– invoice number? send a copy? pay within 5 days?
3 I'm very sorry to hear that.	– order number? check with transporter?
4 We're going somewhere exotic.	– where? how? how long? where / stay?
5 No, I don't.	– how / work? how much / cost? send information?
6 One moment. I'll just check.	– place order? when / deliver? total cost?
7 Yes. Up to my eyeballs.	– help? answer the phone? coffee?

2 With a partner, try and develop each conversation in **1**. Use the conversation ideas below to help you.

A *Who do you think will buy it?*
B *I'm sure children will love it.*
A *Do you think old people will buy it?*
B *Yes, because it's easier to look after than a real dog,* etc.

FOCUS ON BUSINESS ISSUES: The paperless office

1 Complete the questionnaire, then discuss your answers with a partner.

1 How many of the following do you receive and / or send each day?
personal emails: receive .... send ....
professional emails: receive .... send ....

2 How many emails do you print out every day? ....
And how many Internet pages? ....

3 How many printed letters or memos do you receive each day? ....

4 What effect will the Internet have on the amount of post sent by 'snail mail'?
....

5 Could you reduce the amount of paper you print out? If so, how? ....

2 6.4 Listen to the manager of a company which makes printers. Are these statements true (T) or false (F), according to the speakers?

1 We are using less paper now than before. ....
2 We will use more paper in the future. ....
3 There will never be a 'paperless office'. ....
4 We'll make more use of 'snail mail' in the future. ....
5 We'll continue to make paper copies of electronic documents. ....
6 Electronic books will replace traditional books. ....

3 6.4 Listen again. Say what these numbers refer to, as in the example.
88m is the amount of paper produced by an average American company in one year.
a 88m b 1–3% c 6–8% d 40% e 33

4 What three reasons does the manager give for people's 'love affair' with paper?

5 Discuss these questions in pairs or groups.
1 Do you think you are using more paper now than ever before?
2 Do you agree with the manager's predictions in **2** (statements 2–6)? Why / why not?

END-OF-UNIT QUIZ

This is the end of Unit 6. Try this quick quiz to make sure you have understood everything.

1 Who sends these documents, and in what order are they sent? Label them C (customer) or S (supplier) and number them from 1–6.
invoice .... *letter of enquiry* .... *quotation* ....
reminder .... *cheque* .... *order form* ....

2 Answer these questions.
a When do you think you'll retire?
b How are you going to improve your English after this course?

3 Here are some verbs. What are the noun forms?
to deliver *to process* *to produce* *to purchase* *to ship*

4 Complete the gaps with one word.
a I'm sorry *a*................................ that.
b I'm *a*................................ I can't help you.
c *S*................................ I help you with the photocopying?
d Yes, please, if you *c*................................

5 How many verbs can you think of to complete this sentence?
We .... the order yesterday.

07 Presenting information
Workplaces

FOCUS ON WORDS

1 Look at this cartoon. What is *your* job title? What exactly do *you* do in your job?

2 Which departments in the box are responsible for the activities in 1–9 below?

Production	Public Relations	Purchasing	Human Resources	Accounts
Research & Development	Quality Control	Sales & Marketing	Legal	

1 Paying invoices and setting budgets ....
2 Recruiting staff ....
3 Testing new products ....
4 Checking the standard of finished products ....
5 Buying ....
6 Talking to the press ....
7 Checking contracts ....
8 Increasing the number of clients ....
9 Running the factory ....

3 Which department in **2** above do these people usually work in?

1 cost accountants
2 laboratory technicians
3 lawyers
4 representatives (reps)
5 training manager
6 machine operators

4 7.1 PMP is a company which manufactures security doors and gates. You are going to hear some of PMP's employees talking about their jobs.

1 What do they do?

a .... c .... e ....
b .... d .... f ....

2 Which departments do you think they work in?

5 Now work with a partner and answer these questions about your own job.

1 Which department do you work in?
2 Which department(s) do you have most contact with? Why?

6 7.2 You are going to hear a presentation about the company structure of PMP. Listen carefully and complete the organization chart below.

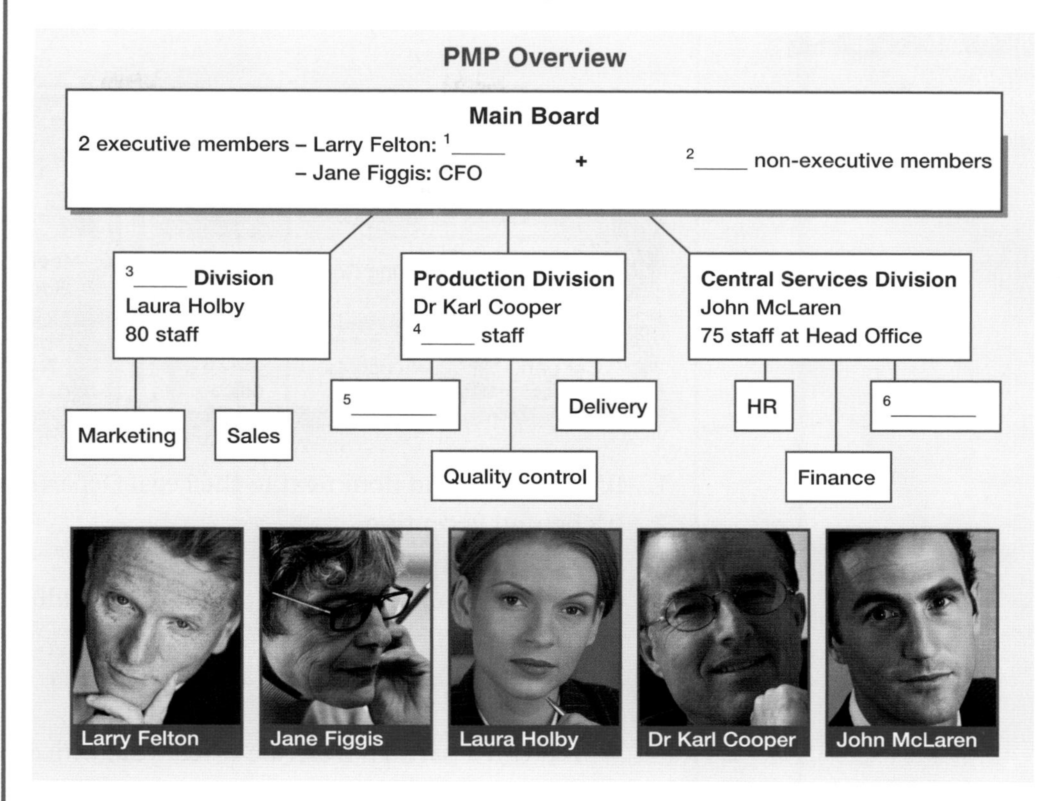

7 7.2 Listen to the presentation again and match 1–5 to a–e to form sentences.

1 Laura is responsible
2 Dr Karl Cooper is in charge
3 There are seven people
4 Sales and Marketing are part
5 The Main Board is responsible to

a the shareholders.
b of the Commercial Division.
c of Production.
d for the Commercial Division.
e on the Main Board.

8 Complete these sentences using a word from the box.

into for of to for in

1 Dr Karl Cooper is in charge .... the Production Division.
2 395 people work .... PMP.
3 The Commercial Division is responsible .... advertising and promotion.
4 The market is divided .... three regions.
5 The head of the Accounts Department reports .... Jane Figgis.
6 Mike Saunders works .... the HR Department.

9 Draw an organization chart for your company. Describe it to your partner.

KEY WORDS

department division be in charge of legal be part of production purchasing quality control report to be responsible for set a budget

FOCUS ON GRAMMAR: Question types

1 Look at this company layout and say what departments are described below.

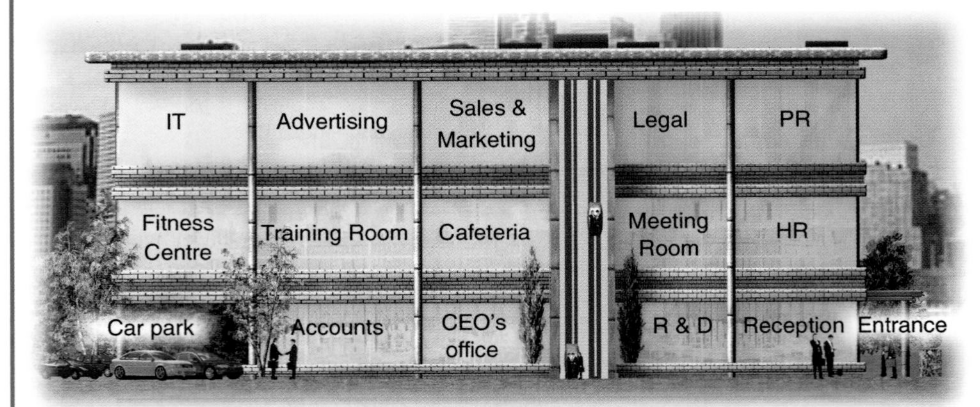

1 It's on the second floor next to the Legal Department.
2 It's behind Reception.
3 It's below Sales and Marketing.
4 It's on the ground floor at the back of the building.
5 It's in the middle of the first floor.
6 It's between the fitness centre and the cafeteria.

2 Work with a partner. Describe where your office / desk is in your building.

3 7.3 A member of the PR team is showing some visitors around the company.
1 Listen and say where they are.
2 Listen again and complete the gaps in the extracts below.

Visitor 1 Excuse me. [1] .... here?

Visitor 1 [2] .... at the moment?
Employee [3] .... We are looking for people to work in the Customer Relations Department.
Visitor 1 [4] .... responsible .... ?

Employee www.kazoo.com. It's easy to remember, [5] .... ?
Visitor 1 The reps spend most days visiting clients, [6] .... ? [7] .... come here?

Visitor 2 [8] .... British?
Employee [9] .... In fact he's German.
Visitor 1 But it's a British company, [10] .... ?

KEY GRAMMAR
With question words (*what*, etc.) we put the auxiliary verb after the question word.
*Where **does** she work?*
To answer a yes / no question we use the same auxiliary verb as in the question.
***Does** she speak German? No, she **doesn't**.*

For more on forming questions, see Language reference page 119.

4 Place the questions from **3** under these headings, as in the example.

WH- QUESTIONS	*YES/NO* QUESTIONS	SENTENCES WITH QUESTION TAGS
		It's easy to remember, isn't it?

KEY GRAMMAR

Question tags are used to check information. To form them we use the same auxiliary verb as in the sentence. If the sentence is positive, the tag is negative and vice versa.

*They **won't** come, **will** they?*

*They **can** fix it, **can't** they?*

If there is no auxiliary verb, we use *do* or *did*.

*She **works** at the hospital, **doesn't** she?*

*They **didn't go** home, **did** they?*

For more on question tags, see Language reference page 120.

5 Complete these sentences using the appropriate form of the verb.

1 She came by plane, *didn't she* ?
2 They don't work here, ...?
3 You .... help them, can't you?
4 We sent the goods last week, ...?
5 He's phoned twice, ...?
6 You won't be here later, ...?
7 You .... been here before, haven't you?
8 I paid last time, ...?

6 Complete the questionnaire about workplaces.

1 Put the words in the right order for each question.
2 Work with a partner. Ask each other the questions and complete the questionnaire.

First complete this information and then check it.

NAME: ________________ NATIONALITY: ____________

COMPANY: ____________ JOB: ____________________

1 kind what in do you work of building? Old ❑ Modern ❑
2 do where work you? Town centre ❑ Outside town ❑
3 other companies with building do share the you? Yes ❑ No ❑
4 work how there many people? ____________________
5 workplace does what have facilities your? ____________________
6 leisure it facilities does what have? ____________________
7 office you an do share? Yes ❑ No ❑ (If no, go to question 9.)
8 do how it many share with people you ? ____________________
9 the is about best what workplace thing your? ____________________
10 … and the worst? ____________________

FOCUS ON EXPRESSIONS: Presenting information

1 What makes a good presentation?

2 7.4 Listen to the opening of a presentation and answer these questions.

1 What's the speaker's job?
2 What is Chupa Chups?
3 How many parts are there in his presentation?
4 What four topics is he going to talk about?

3 7.4 How does Johan Hedborg introduce each point? Listen again and match the expressions in A, B, and C to make complete sentences.

A	B	C
Firstly,	I'll look at	the structure.
Then,	I'm going to tell you a little bit about	their international activity.
After that,	I'll talk about	the history of the company.
Finally,	I'm going to talk about	its sales performance.

4 Your boss has asked you to talk about your department to a group of new employees. Choose four different aspects to talk about, then introduce them, using the language in **3**.

5 7.5 Listen to Part 2 of the talk and complete the slide below.

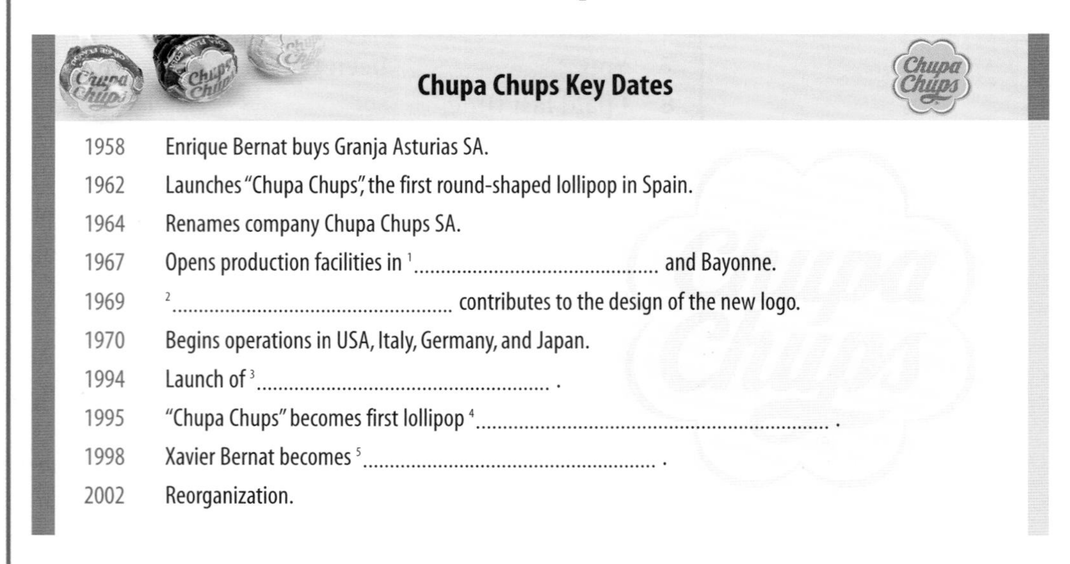

6 7.5 Listen again to Part 2 of the talk and complete the gaps.

1 .... at this slide.
2 .... some of the key years in the history of Chupa Chups.
3 .... see that?
4 .... , the company continued to expand internationally in the 70s and 80s.
5 Now, ... move on?

7 You are going to present a slide to a partner. Use the language in **6** to help you. Student A, turn to File 14 on page 90. Student B, turn to File 14 on page 98.

8 Look at this bar chart. Choose the correct alternative in *italics*.

1 There was an *upward / downward* trend in sales over a ten-year period.
2 Sales almost *doubled / halved* in the five years from 1996 to 2001.
3 The *vertical / horizontal* axis represents sales in millions of euros.
4 Between 1997 and 1999, sales *rose / fell / stayed the same*.

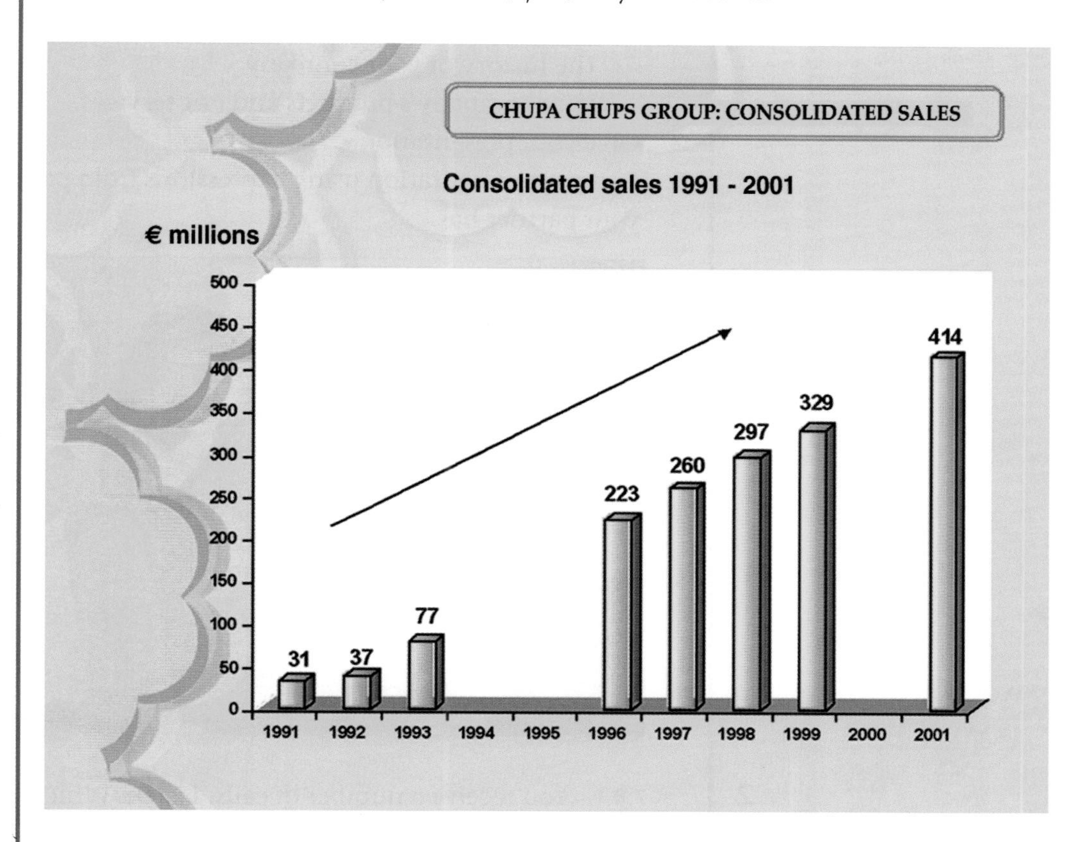

9 (((7.6))) Listen to Part 3 of the talk and complete the information on the chart.

10 (((7.7))) Now listen to Part 4 where the speaker finishes his talk. What does the speaker say at the end? Put these words in the correct order.

1 my end me that talk the brings to of ....
2 listening very thanks for much ....
3 you I it useful hope was for ....
4 any anybody have questions does? ....

KEY EXPRESSIONS

Introducing talk: *I'm here today to tell you about ...* *Firstly, I'm going to tell you about ...* *Then / Next I'll look at ...* *Finally, I'll talk about ...*

Referring to visuals: *Have a look at this slide.* *This graph / diagram / table / slide shows ...* *Can everybody see that?* *As you can see ...*

Describing trends: *It's risen / fallen / stayed the same.* *It rose / fell / stayed the same.* *There was a downward / upward trend.* *Sales have halved / doubled ...* *The vertical / horizontal axis represents ...*

FOCUS ON COMMUNICATION

1 You are going to take it in turns to give a short presentation to your partner.

1. Choose one of these subjects and tell your partner which subject you have chosen. Your partner should write down some questions to ask you after the presentation. The subjects are:
   - the department you work in
   - the building you work in
   - the organizational structure of your company
   - the history of your company
   - your company's products and / or services.
2. Give your presentation.
3. End your presentation using expressions from page 57. Deal with any questions your partner has.

2 7.8 You receive a number of calls. Listen. Which departments are they for?

1 .... 3 .... 5 ....
2 .... 4 ....

3 Read this email. Now write a similar email giving directions to your office.

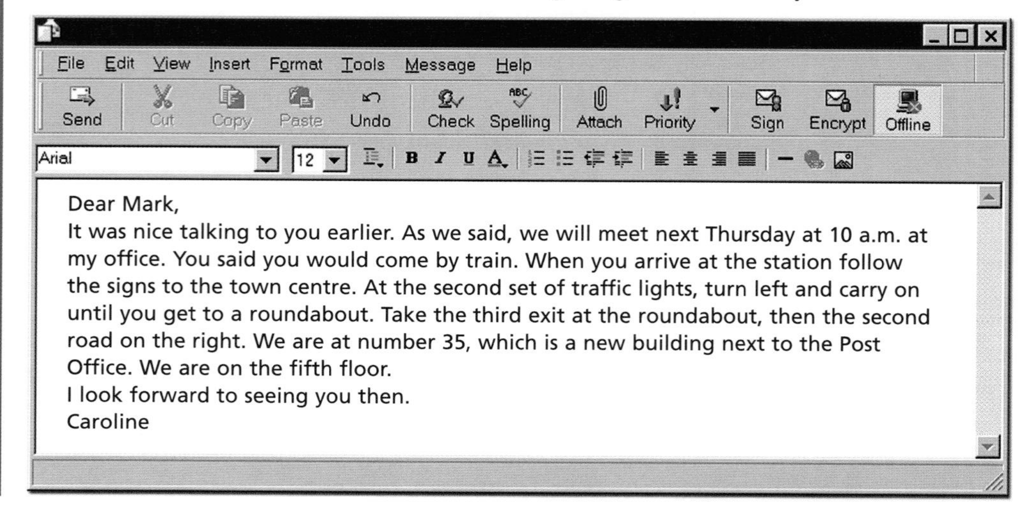

Dear Mark,
It was nice talking to you earlier. As we said, we will meet next Thursday at 10 a.m. at my office. You said you would come by train. When you arrive at the station follow the signs to the town centre. At the second set of traffic lights, turn left and carry on until you get to a roundabout. Take the third exit at the roundabout, then the second road on the right. We are at number 35, which is a new building next to the Post Office. We are on the fifth floor.
I look forward to seeing you then.
Caroline

FOCUS ON BUSINESS ISSUES: Teleworking

1 Think of people who *don't* work in an office. Where do they work?

2 Read this short article about an unusual workplace.

COLLETTA DI CASTELBIANCO is a small, 12th-century Italian village, high up in the hills. In 1970 there was just *one* person living there! Twenty years later a group of architects bought the village to build holiday apartments. Then, in 1996, Telecom Italia installed a fibre-optic cable and suddenly Colletta was connected to the rest of the world via the Internet. From that day on, scientists, lawyers, accountants and designers have chosen it as the perfect workplace. Teleworkers choose to live there in beautiful surroundings and visit their companies and customers from time to time by car or plane.

3 (((7.9))) You are going to hear a resident of Colletta discussing her lifestyle. Listen and answer these questions.

1 What jobs do she and her husband do?
2 Does she work more at home or in London?
3 Do the people in the village speak Italian?
4 Why is it a friendly place to live?
5 How expensive is it to live there?

4 Work with a partner. Would you like to live in Colletta? What are the advantages and disadvantages of working from home?

END-OF-UNIT QUIZ

This is the end of Unit 7. Try this quick quiz to make sure you have understood everything.

1 Which departments in a company are represented by these intials: PR, HR?
2 Name five other company departments.
3 Complete these sentences with question tags.
   a You're French, ...?
   b You work here, ...?
   c She's the Marketing Director, ...?
4 Make a question from these words.
   company work for which she does?
5 What would you say to start a presentation?
6 How would you end one?
7 Write the opposite of these words:
   a upward ....
   b horizontal ....
   c rise ....
   d stay the same ....

Entertaining
Food and drink

FOCUS ON WORDS

1 Look at the pictures. What are these people having for lunch? What do you usually have for lunch and where do you eat? What do visitors to your company have for lunch? Where do they go to eat?

2 What kind of things would you expect to eat in these countries: England, Spain, China, France, Japan, Thailand, America, India, Italy?

3 What adjectives in A would you use to describe the food in B? There is sometimes more than one possibility.

A	B
healthy	potatoes
simple	chips
tasty	chocolate
spicy	garlic bread
greasy	salad
filling	carrots
crunchy	cheese sandwich
sweet	curry

4 Work with a partner. Add as many more items as you can to each list.

1 Ways of cooking *to roast, to fry,* ....
2 Vegetables *potatoes, carrots,* ....
3 Desserts *apple pie, fruit salad,* ....
4 Meats *pork, veal,* ....
5 Cutlery *teaspoon, knife,* ....
6 Fish and seafood *trout, prawns,* ....
7 Dairy products *milk, cheese,* ....

5 Look at the illustration.

1 Work with a partner. Match the words in the box to a–i. Are any of these difficult to eat? Why?

2 What other things do you find difficult to eat?

oysters soft-boiled egg asparagus prawns corn on the cob cherry tomatoes caviar spaghetti lobster

6 8.1 Listen to a host and guest discussing the menu in a restaurant.

1 Tick (✓) four of the dishes they discuss in this list.

Greek salad ❑
scampi ❑
steak ❑
lasagne ❑
ravioli ❑
curry ❑
pizza ❑
soup ❑

2 What is *scampi*?

3 What do they decide to order?

7 Work with a partner. A visitor is coming to your region. Think of a typical three-course meal to offer him / her. Describe your menu to your partner, explaining what the dishes are and how they are cooked.

KEY WORDS

crunchy cutlery dairy desserts filling fry greasy healthy roast simple spicy sweet tasty vegetarian

FOCUS ON EXPRESSIONS 1: Restaurant language

1 Look at the expressions in 1–10. Who says them in a restaurant – the waiter or the customer? Write *W* (waiter) or *C* (customer) beside each question, as in the example.

1 Could I have a table for three, please? C
2 What do you recommend? ....
3 Are you ready to order? ....
4 What is the soup of the day? ....
5 How would you like it cooked? ....
6 Who's having the fish? ....
7 Could I have a glass, please? ....
8 Would you like to taste it? ....
9 Anything else? ....
10 Could I have the bill? ....

2 8.2 Think of possible replies to each of the remarks in **1**. Then, listen and compare your answers.

3 Match the expressions in A to the descriptions in B.

A		B	
1	Bon appétit!	a	Say this before your first drink.
2	It's delicious!	b	Say this before you eat.
3	Let me get this.	c	Ask about someone's food.
4	Cheers!	d	Say something tastes very good.
5	How's yours?	e	Say something is not very good.
6	It's a bit cold / over-cooked.	f	Offer to pay.

4 Work with a partner. Have short conversations using these prompts. When you have finished, change roles.

1
Customer: Ask for a table.
Waiter: The restaurant is full. Offer a table in an hour.
Customer: Ask about the bar.
Waiter: Show the way to the bar.

2
Waiter: Ask about ordering.
Customer: Ask for more time.
Waiter: Ask about drinks.
Customer: Order a bottle of house white and a bottle of water.
Waiter: Ask about the water.

3
Customer: Ask your guest if their food is OK.
Guest: You aren't happy. It's cold.
Customer: Suggest ordering something different.

4
Customer: Ask about the bill.
Waiter: Give the bill.
Customer: Ask about paying by credit card.
Waiter: Agree.

FOCUS ON GRAMMAR 1: 1st conditional

1 What criteria do you consider when choosing a restaurant to entertain a guest?

2 8.3 Three people are discussing where to take some visitors for dinner. Listen to the conversation and complete the table below.

RESTAURANT	BENITO'S	CHAPTER TWO
Type of food	Continental	1 ....
Price range	€35–40 per head	2 € ....
Entertainment	Singer every night	3 ....
Opening times	4 ....–11.30 p.m.	7.30 p.m.–10.30 p.m.

3 8.4 Listen to sentences from the conversation again and complete the gaps.

1 If we .... Chapter Two, ... cost us about €400.
2 If it .... a nice evening, we .... able to sit outside.
3 But if it ...., it .... be nicer at Benito's.
4 If we .... to Chapter Two on Thursday, there .... live jazz.
5 It .... be full if we .... there for just after 7.00.

KEY GRAMMAR

We use the 1st conditional when something will probably happen. We form it like this:

If + present simple, *will/won't* + verb.

***If** we **go** to Chapter Two, it **will be** an expensive evening.*

*If he **doesn't know**, he **won't be** angry.*

For more on the 1st conditional, see Language reference page 107.

4 Work with a partner. For each situation below, one of you asks a question using *if* and the other replies, as in the example.

A *If you cut your prices, what will the customers think?*
B *Our customers will be very happy if we cut our prices.*

SITUATION	QUESTION	REPLY
1 You want to cut your prices.	Customers think?	Be happy.
2 Your flight to Paris may be cancelled.	Get to Paris?	Rent a car.
3 You want to close a department.	How staff react?	Be very worried.
4 You want to move your office out of town.	Benefits?	Easier to park.

FOCUS ON EXPRESSIONS 2: Likes and dislikes

1 What do you do in your free time?

2 Four people are discussing their likes and dislikes.

1 8.5 Listen and write down the things they do / don't like doing.

	LIKES	DISLIKES
Michael	cinema - American action films	
Jessica		
Stella		
Tom		

2 8.5 Listen again. Complete the scale below with the expressions they use to talk about their likes and dislikes.

3 What form of the verb do we use after these expressions?

3 Look at this list of activities and decide how much you like them.

1 Rank them from 0 (hate) to 5 (love).

- ❒ Attending meetings
- ❒ Going to conferences
- ❒ Working under pressure
- ❒ Emptying my in-tray
- ❒ Using the telephone
- ❒ Meeting visitors
- ❒ Travelling on business
- ❒ Working at the weekend
- ❒ Working alone
- ❒ Dealing with emails
- ❒ Preparing reports
- ❒ Entertaining customers

2 Compare your ranking with your partner's. Give reasons for your ranking.

KEY EXPRESSIONS

I love ... (verb + -ing) *I really like / I'm keen on / I'm fond of ... (verb + -ing)* *I quite like / I don't mind ... (verb + -ing)*
I'm not very keen on / I don't really like ... (verb + -ing) *I don't like ... (verb + -ing)* *I hate / I can't stand ... (verb + -ing)*

FOCUS ON GRAMMAR 2: 2nd conditional

1 Say what you would do in these situations, as in the example.
If someone offered me insects to eat, I would say, 'Sorry, I'm a vegetarian.'

1 If you were on a business trip in a foreign country and your host offered you insects to eat, what would you do?

2 If you were eating with an important customer and you knocked red wine over their clothes, what would you do?

3 If you took a client to a very expensive restaurant and then discovered you had no money and the restaurant refused your credit card, what would you do?

4 If you were a guest at your manager's house and they gave you a dessert that was impossible to eat, what would you do?

KEY GRAMMAR

We use the 2nd conditional to talk about something that will probably not happen.

We form it like this: *If* + past simple, *would/wouldn't* + verb.

***If I was** late for an important meeting, I **would make** an excuse.*

***If I was** rich, I **wouldn't need** to work.*

For more on the 2nd conditional, see Language reference page 108.

2 You are going to hear an extract from a training seminar.

1 8.6 Listen. What are the two difficult situations?

2 8.6 Listen again and complete these sentences.

a If he .... something like that I .... say, 'Some other time maybe.'

b If they .... me to sing, I .... know what to say.

3 What would you say in these situations?

3 Work with a partner. Complete the sentences below.

1 If my boss retired, ...
2 If I retired early, ...
3 I would be happier if ....
4 If I were you, ...
5 I would probably earn more money if ....
6 If I had more time at work, ...
7 If I had more money, ...

FOCUS ON COMMUNICATION

1 Work with a partner. Student A, you are entertaining a foreign client, Student B, next week. Your information is below. Student B, turn to File 17 on page 99.

1 Your visitor is arriving at 4 p.m. You have a budget of €250 and 24 hours to plan. Look at the list of possibilities below and phone your visitor to plan the day. Without giving prices, encourage him / her to choose activities which will fit within your budget, as in the examples.
Would you like to go to the theatre?
If we went to the evening concert, we wouldn't have time ...

Hotels	**Cost**	**Time**
Grand Hotel **** (modern, outside city)	€150	
Aston Hotel *** (traditional, outside city)	€120	
Barley Hotel ** (modern, very central)	€80	
Food		
Snack lunch in Benton's Wine Bar	€15	(1 hour)
Full lunch at the Astoria Steakhouse	€40	(2 hours)
Dinner in Bon Appétit (French)	€50	(2 hours)
Dinner in Dino's (Italian)	€30	(2 hours)
Activities		
Guided tour of the city	€20	(2 hours)
Attending tennis match	€45	(3 hours)
Playing golf as a guest in your club	€10	(2 hours)
Trip to famous historical building in countryside	€45 (including taxi)	(3 hours)
Visit to new modern art gallery	€15	(1–2 hours)
Shopping	free	(1–2 hours)
Theatre	€35 (afternoon) €50 (evening)	(3 hours)
Concert	€30 (evening)	(2 hours)

2 Add up the total cost. Are you within budget?

2 Read this email.

1 Why is JJ writing to their guest? What will they do if the weather is bad?

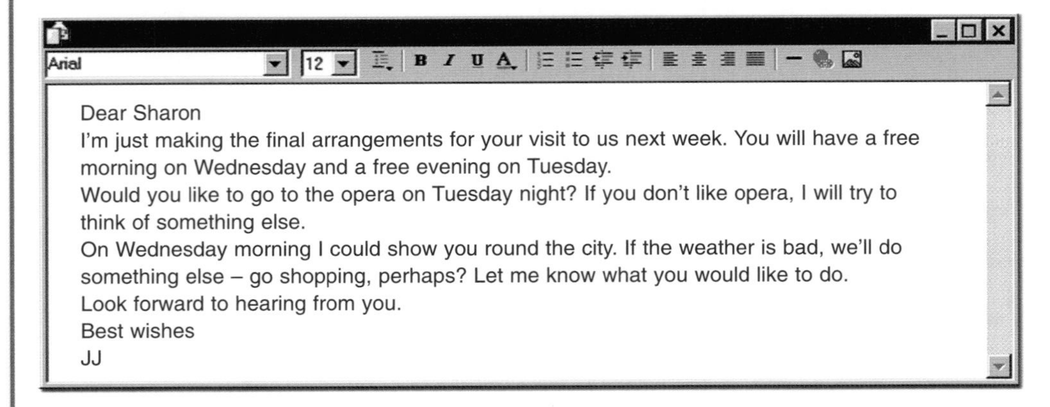
Dear Sharon
I'm just making the final arrangements for your visit to us next week. You will have a free morning on Wednesday and a free evening on Tuesday.
Would you like to go to the opera on Tuesday night? If you don't like opera, I will try to think of something else.
On Wednesday morning I could show you round the city. If the weather is bad, we'll do something else – go shopping, perhaps? Let me know what you would like to do.
Look forward to hearing from you.
Best wishes
JJ

2 Now write a similar email to your partner, inviting them to do some things around your town.

FOCUS ON BUSINESS ISSUES: Entertaining clients

1 If you wanted to make a good impression on a customer, what would you do? Does your company have a budget for entertaining clients? Have you ever been invited to a sports event or a concert by a business contact?

2 8.7 Listen to this discussion about corporate entertainment.

1 What two events does Simon want to organize?
2 Who are they for and how much will they cost?
3 Why does Isobel say, 'I'm not convinced'?
4 How does Simon justify spending the money?
5 Does Isobel accept Simon's arguments in the end?
6 Who do you agree with? Why?

3 One of your suppliers wants to invite you to an event. Put the activities below in order of preference. Then, discuss your reasons with a partner.

- Three-hour balloon flight
- A gourmet meal at a top restaurant
- A day at the horse races
- An evening at the opera
- A private viewing at an art gallery
- A day at a Formula 1 Grand Prix

END-OF-UNIT QUIZ

This is the end of Unit 8. Try this quick quiz to make sure you have understood everything.

1 Name five ways of cooking.
2 What do we call the three courses in a restaurant?
3 Make a conditional sentence from these words:
   a another spoke if language she salesperson would a perfect be she
   b car wouldn't work time didn't if I to get have I on a
   c get I'll London if job to move the I
   d if resign don't promotion get I I'll a
4 What do you say:
   a as you start eating?
   b to your guest after a minute or two?
   c to the waiter at the end of the meal?
5 How do you feel about football? opera? heavy-metal music? long novels?
6 Which is the odd one out:
   a A waitress B cooker C chef D barman
   b A lettuce B broccoli C peach D spinach
   c A knife B glass C spoon D fork

09 Taking part in meetings
Advertising and selling

WORDS
Advertising and promotions

GRAMMAR
Modals of obligation and permission

EXPRESSIONS 1
Managing discussions

EXPRESSIONS 2
Describing trends

COMMUNICATION
A meeting about advertising strategy
Writing the minutes of a meeting

BUSINESS ISSUES
Different types of meeting

END-OF-UNIT QUIZ

FOCUS ON WORDS

1 Complete the questionnaire. Then, work with a partner and explain your answers.

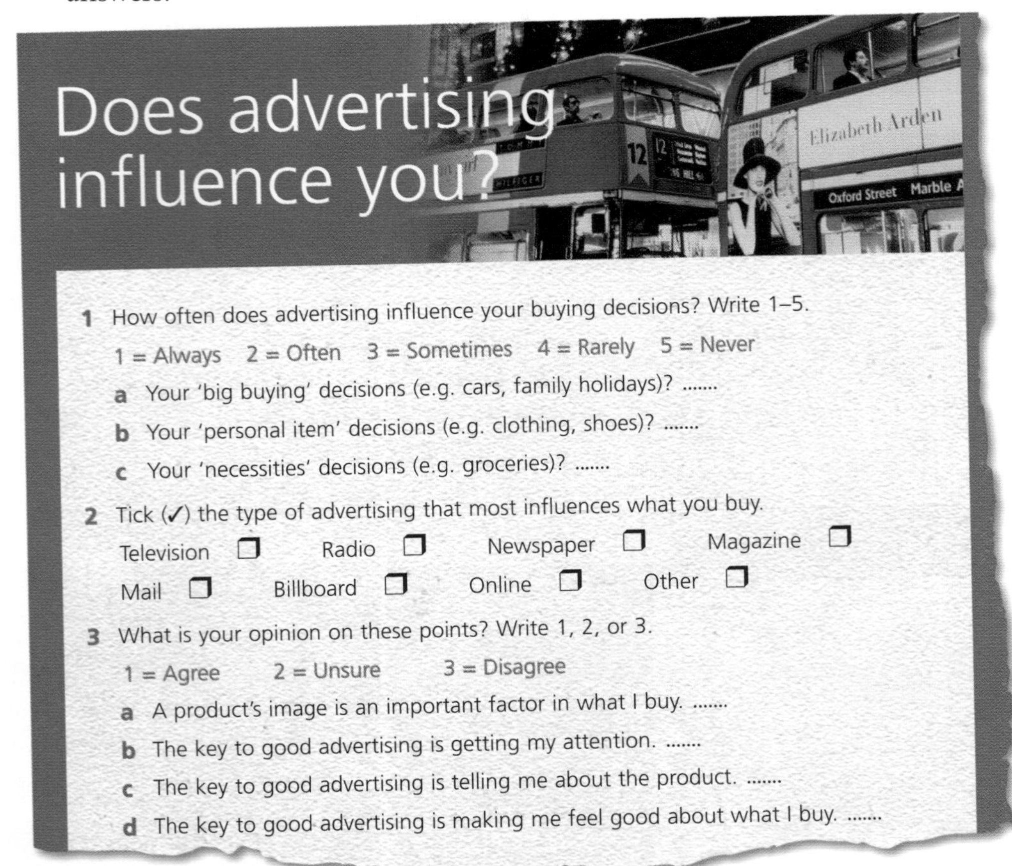

Does advertising influence you?

1 How often does advertising influence your buying decisions? Write 1–5.
1 = Always 2 = Often 3 = Sometimes 4 = Rarely 5 = Never
a Your 'big buying' decisions (e.g. cars, family holidays)? ....
b Your 'personal item' decisions (e.g. clothing, shoes)? ....
c Your 'necessities' decisions (e.g. groceries)? ....

2 Tick (✓) the type of advertising that most influences what you buy.
Television ❒ Radio ❒ Newspaper ❒ Magazine ❒
Mail ❒ Billboard ❒ Online ❒ Other ❒

3 What is your opinion on these points? Write 1, 2, or 3.
1 = Agree 2 = Unsure 3 = Disagree
a A product's image is an important factor in what I buy. ....
b The key to good advertising is getting my attention. ....
c The key to good advertising is telling me about the product. ....
d The key to good advertising is making me feel good about what I buy. ....

2 Complete this diagram with the words in the box, as in the example. Some words can go in more than one category. Add any more words you can think of.

TV *catalogues* kiosks single people free samples professionals posters billboards bus shelters brochures sponsorship banner adverts promotional video / DVD leaflets radio the general public word-of-mouth

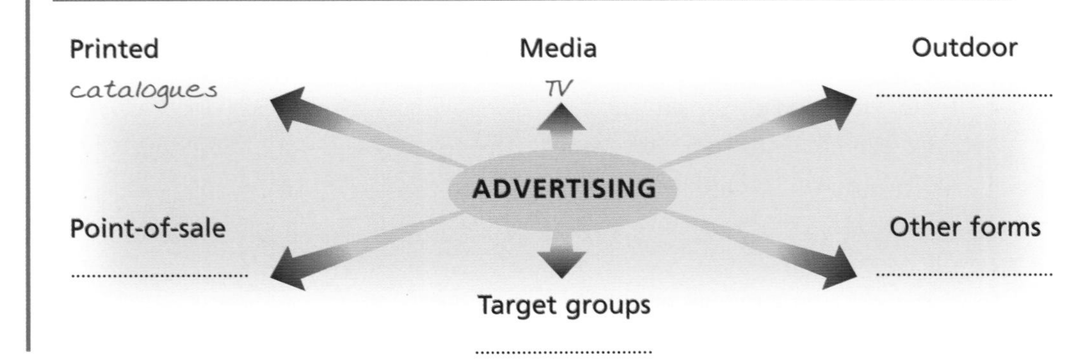

3 How does your company advertise? What sort of customers do you target?

4 Every week *USA Today* looks at how much consumers like advertising campaigns. Read the article below and answer these questions.

1 What kind of people do you think buy a product like this?
2 Would their advertising campaign have appealed to you? Why / why not?

Kodak Advantix Preview camera

Product features and benefits

SPECIAL FEATURE:
Screen which allows you to see your photo after taking it.

BENEFITS:
Users know they have the exact picture they want and don't waste money on printing useless photos.

Advertising campaign

DESCRIPTION OF ADVERTISEMENT / COMMERCIAL:
Shows a couple visiting a small French town who are trying to reproduce an old family photo taken in the same place many years ago. They finally manage to take a perfect picture after a number of mistakes. Without the Advantix Preview, they wouldn't have seen the results until after their holiday, when it would have been too late.

SLOGAN:
'Share moments. Share life.'

RESPONSE TO CAMPAIGN FROM KEY TARGET GROUPS:
24% of men, 39% of women 'liked it a lot' (average response is 22%).

5 Find words in the text to complete these questions, as in the example. The first letter is given.

1 Is the *a*dvertisement....... on TV, on the radio, or in a newspaper or magazine?
2 Who are the main *t*.............................. groups or consumers?
3 What are the main *f*.............................. or characteristics of the product?
4 What are the *b*.............................. of the product to the consumer?
5 Does the advertisement use any memorable phrases or *s*..............................?
6 Do you think the advertising *c*.............................. is a good one? Why / why not?

6 Think of an advertisement which you really like. Then, work with a partner and ask each other the questions in **5**.

KEY WORDS

benefits billboards brochures campaign features free samples point-of-sale promotional slogans sponsorship target groups word-of-mouth

FOCUS ON GRAMMAR: Modals of obligation and permission

1 Do you think there is too much advertising in your country? Are there any products advertised that you think shouldn't be advertised?

2 Read the text about advertising rules in Japan. Which words in *italics* refer to:

- what you can do?
- what you can't do?
- what is necessary?

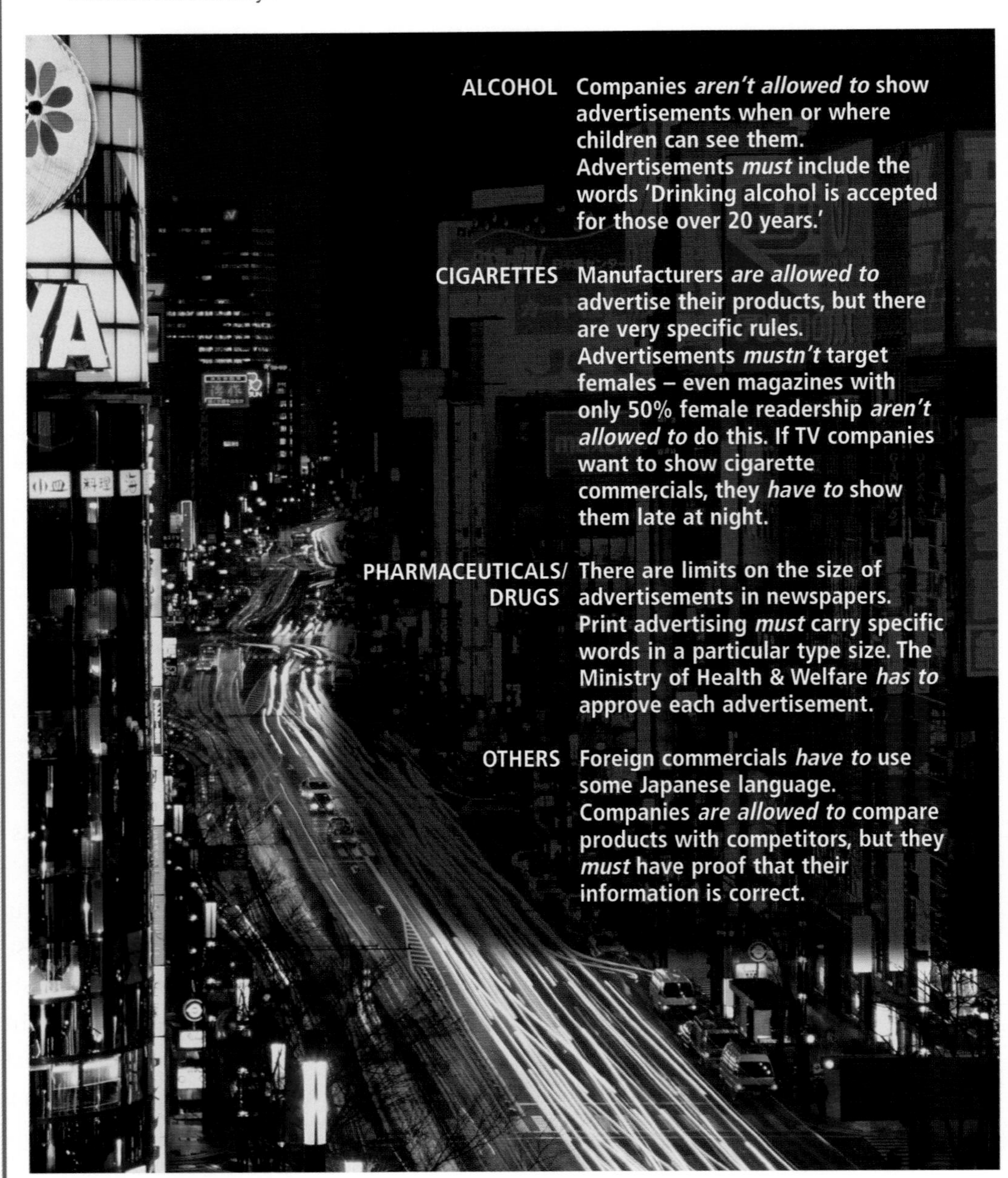

ALCOHOL Companies *aren't allowed to* show advertisements when or where children can see them. Advertisements *must* include the words 'Drinking alcohol is accepted for those over 20 years.'

CIGARETTES Manufacturers *are allowed to* advertise their products, but there are very specific rules. Advertisements *mustn't* target females – even magazines with only 50% female readership *aren't allowed to* do this. If TV companies want to show cigarette commercials, they *have to* show them late at night.

PHARMACEUTICALS/DRUGS There are limits on the size of advertisements in newspapers. Print advertising *must* carry specific words in a particular type size. The Ministry of Health & Welfare *has to* approve each advertisement.

OTHERS Foreign commercials *have to* use some Japanese language. Companies *are allowed to* compare products with competitors, but they *must* have proof that their information is correct.

3 Read the text aloud with a partner, using alternatives for the expressions in *italics*, as in the example.

*Manufacturers **are allowed to advertise** their products.*
*Manufacturers **can advertise** their products.*

4 (((9.1))) Listen to a Thai businessman talking about advertising rules in Thailand, and complete the notes.

Foreign commercials: You [1] .... show them, but the voices [2] .... in Thai.
Words on TV or on packaging [3] .... in Thai.
Commercials with foreign songs: Advertisers [4] .... translate them.
Taboo subjects: You [5] .... refer to religion.
Alcohol: You [6] .... show commercials for alcoholic drinks.
Commercials [7] .... include pictures of people drinking.
Cigarettes: You [8] .... advertise them at all.
Comparative advertising: Companies [9] .... make specific comparisons with their competitors.

KEY GRAMMAR

Not have to means something is not necessary.

*You **don't have to** email the report. You can send it by post.*

Mustn't means do not / you are not allowed to do something.

*Companies **mustn't** make comparisons with their competitors. It's illegal.*

For more on modals of obligation and permission, see Language reference page 111.

5 Complete these sentences with *must*, *mustn't*, or *don't have to*.

1 You .... advertise cigarettes on TV in many countries.
2 You .... help me – I can do it myself.
3 All visitors .... show proof of identity before entering the building.
4 You .... go in that room because it contains dangerous chemicals.
5 I .... work at weekends – only from Monday to Friday.
6 I .... go to the post office before it closes.

6 (((9.2))) Now listen to these sentences about advertising in Sri Lanka. Do you hear *can* or *can't*? Practise saying the sentences.

1 You .... advertise alcohol on TV.
2 You .... show alcohol adverts at the cinema.
3 Cigarette companies .... advertise in newspapers.
4 You .... show cigarette commercials on TV.
5 Cigarette commercials .... be shown at the cinema.
6 You .... compare your products with your competitors'.

7 With a partner, ask and answer questions about advertising rules in your country. Use the language in the box and the sentences in **4** and **5** to help you.

Can you ...? Are you allowed to ...? Do you have to ...? I'm not sure, but I think ...

- WORDS
  Advertising and promotions
- GRAMMAR
  Modals of obligation and permission
- **EXPRESSIONS 1**
  Managing discussions
- EXPRESSIONS 2
  Describing trends
- COMMUNICATION
  A meeting about advertising strategy
  Writing the minutes of a meeting
- BUSINESS ISSUES
  Different types of meeting
- END-OF-UNIT QUIZ

FOCUS ON EXPRESSIONS 1: Managing discussions

1 Do you spend too much time in meetings? Why are meetings sometimes too long?

2 9.3 Three managers of Fitstart, a sports-shoe manufacturer, are discussing a new sales campaign in Central Europe. Listen and complete the notes below.

Advertising:
- *Budget last year:* ....
- *Money spent last year:* ....
- *Budget this year:* ....
- *Extra money to be used for:* ....

Sales:
- *This year's target: +* ....%
- *Next two years: +* ....%
- *Countries to target: the Czech Republic,* ...., ...
- *Recruitment:* .... *new sales reps*

3 9.3 The sentences in B were said just after those in A. Match the sentences, then listen and check.

A
1. Right. Thank you for coming today.
2. Sorry, I didn't catch that.
3. That's not really on the agenda for today.
4. OK, I think we've covered advertising.
5. Sorry, I'm not with you.
6. I think that's everything for today.

B
- a Can we sum up what we've agreed?
- b Could you be more specific?
- c Could you go over those figures again?
- d Can we start? We're here today to discuss ...
- e Can we move on to the next point?
- f Can we come back to that another time?

4 Which expressions in A or B above are used:
1. to begin the meeting? ....
2. to say you didn't hear something? ....
3. to say you didn't understand something? ....
4. to keep to the right subject? ....
5. to change to a new subject? ....
6. to close the meeting? ....

KEY EXPRESSIONS

Can we come back to that another time? Can we move on to the next point? Can we start? We're here today to discuss ... Can we sum up what we've agreed? Could you go over ... again? OK, I think we've covered ... Sorry, I didn't catch that. Sorry, I'm not with you. That's everything for today.

FOCUS ON EXPRESSIONS 2: Describing trends

1 Study the advertising budget bar chart (A) and use the correct form of the words in the box to complete the sentences.

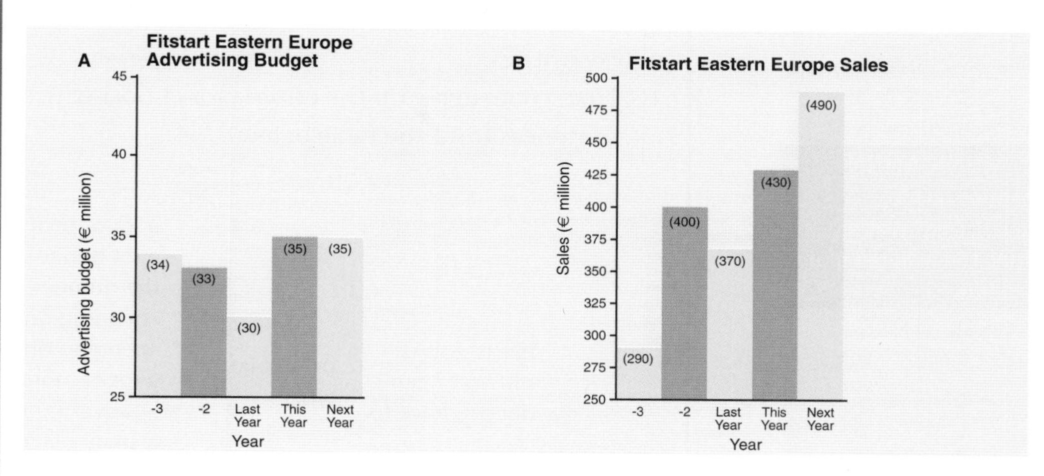

stand at	*rise sharply*	drop slightly	remain stable	increase by	fall to

1 The budget *has risen sharply* this year.
2 It .... five million euros this year.
3 It .... 30 million euros last year.
4 It .... next year.
5 It .... two years ago.
6 It .... 34 million euros three years ago.

2 Now describe the bar chart for sales (B), as in the example.
Three years ago sales stood at 290 million euros. Two years ago they ...

3 Work in groups of three or four. You work for Fitstart in Central Europe. You are meeting to discuss the advertising budget for next year. This is your agenda. Student A, you are the Advertising Manager. Turn to File 15 on page 90. Students B, C, and D, you are sales managers from the different countries. Student B, turn to File 18 on page 99. Student C, turn to File 2 on page 101. Student D, turn to File 4 on page 102.

FITSTART SPORTSWEAR

1 Presentation of sales results for last year
   – *Poland*
   – *Hungary*
   – *Czech Republic*
2 Advertising needs in each country for this year
3 Discussion and decision

KEY EXPRESSIONS

drop slightly *fall to* *increase by* *remain stable* *rise sharply* *stand at*

FOCUS ON COMMUNICATION

1 Work with a partner or in groups. You and your partner(s) work for a book club which sells books to the public by mail order or through your website. You advertise for new members in magazines. You want to open your book club in two new countries.

1 First, try to agree on the criteria for choosing the countries by making sentences from the table below.

It	has to / must mustn't / can't doesn't have to	be a country where	a lot of people live. a lot of books are written. the number of new books is increasing. spending on books is low. spending on books is rising. a lot of money is spent on magazine advertising. a small percentage of advertising is in magazines. the number of Internet users is high. the number of Internet users is going up.

2 Now look at the information in File 5 on page 102. Describe the trends and decide how important they are in relation to the criteria you discussed in **1**.

3 Which two countries are you going to choose, and why? Is there any other information you would need to help you make your decision? Write notes about your decisions.

2 Your boss has asked you to write the minutes of the meeting you had in **1**.

1 Use the notes you took in the meeting to complete the minutes.

2 When you have finished, compare your minutes with the other participants'. Did you all write the same? Try to agree on a final version.

Please let me know if I have left anything out or if you have any amendments.

Minutes: NEW MARKETS MEETING
Date: ______
Present: ______
Apologies: ______
We held the meeting yesterday to decide on ______.
We agreed that ______ and ______ would (probably) be the best new markets.
The reasons for our decision were as follows:
Firstly, ______
Secondly, ______
Thirdly, ______
Finally, ______
Before we make a final decision, we still have to ______.

FOCUS ON BUSINESS ISSUES: Different types of meeting

Open-air meeting

Stand-up meeting

Hotel (or restaurant) meeting

1 The photos show three different types of meetings. What sort of meeting do you think would be good in each location or situation? Explain your reasons.

2 9.4 Listen to two people talking about meetings at work. Which type of meeting in **1** are they talking about?

3 9.4 Listen again. Are these statements true (T) or false (F)?

1. The five-minute meeting must finish after five minutes. ....
2. The meeting starts at six. ....
3. There's no agenda for the meeting. ....
4. It's quicker than exchanging information by email. ....
5. Only the project leader sits down. ....

4 Work with a partner and discuss these questions.

1. Have you tried anything similar to these meetings? Did it / would it work?
2. What's the best time of day to have a meeting? And the best day of the week?
3. Is a meeting better for exchanging information than email?

END-OF-UNIT QUIZ

This is the end of Unit 9. Try this quick quiz to make sure you have understood everything.

1 Match the words in A and B to make two-word expressions.

A	B
target	commercials
advertising	sample
banner	group
TV	campaign
free	adverts

2 Change the verbs and expressions in *italics* without changing the meaning. Each sentence must begin with the word *You* ...

1. You *must* show your security badge at reception.
2. You *aren't allowed to* go in this room.
3. You *can* take a lunch break between 12 and 2 p.m.
4. It's *not necessary for you* to work after 5.30 p.m.

3 Look at the statistics, then describe what happened to the share price, as in the example.
In 2001 the share price fell to $30.

SHARE PRICE FOR T-KAT CONTINENTAL				
2000	2001	2002	2003	2004
$50	$30	$30	$34	$80

4 Choose a word from A and B to complete each question 1–4.

A sum move go come
B on back up over

1. Can we .... to the next point?
2. Can we .... to that another time?
3. Could you .... that again?
4. Can we .... what we've decided?

10 Managing your time
Projects and processes

FOCUS ON WORDS

1 Complete the table, then explain your answers to a partner.

	ALWAYS TRUE	SOMETIMES TRUE	NEVER TRUE
I organize my working time well.	❑	❑	❑
I have a lot of interruptions at work.	❑	❑	❑
When I have important work to do, I finish it on time.	❑	❑	❑

2 Do you think you could manage your time better? Read the text below and choose a title for each paragraph from this list.

Analyse the results
Know when work must be finished
Plan your perfect working day
Find out how long your work takes
Make a daily 'to do' list

TIME MANAGEMENT
FIVE ESSENTIAL STEPS

1 ....

Keep a record of the different tasks you do each day and monitor the time they take. This shows where you lose time. Also record the times when your energy levels are highest and lowest.

2 ....

After a week or two, review your work record and evaluate your use of work time. How can you do the longer tasks more quickly?

3 ....

Prepare a schedule for your ideal working day. Choose two hours of 'high energy time' for doing important or urgent tasks. This should be when you have no or few interruptions.

4 ....

What deadlines do you have? Make sure you have a calendar in your office to mark all the important dates: when tasks have to be done by, meetings, etc. This will show you how much time you have left to complete the different projects.

5 ....

Every morning, make a list of what work you have to do. Schedule the day's tasks, following your 'ideal working day' plan. Keep your list with you, and tick (✓) the different tasks as you do them.

3 Find words in the text that match these definitions. The first letter is given.

1 parts of a process s*teps*..................
2 a piece of work to be done t..................
3 a programme of work s..................
4 a date when something must be finished d..................
5 to look again at something r..................
6 to analyse e..................
7 a list of the details of something r..................

4 Work with a partner. What do you think of the advice in the text? Do you do any of the things mentioned? Why / why not?

5 10.1 A project engineer is describing the process of developing new software. First complete this summary with the words in the box. Then, listen and check your answers. Which expressions are used to introduce each step?

evaluate	schedule	decide	review	steps	record	deadline

1 .... on the different .... in the development process.
2 Prepare a provisional .... for the development of the product.
3 Agree with the customer on the .... for delivery.
4 .... progress at the end of each week.
5 Keep a .... of all delays, with the reasons.
6 Three months after delivery, ... success of development project.

6 Match sentences in A with sentences in B.

A

1 We will finish the project just in time.
2 The meeting started on time.
3 We're ahead of schedule.
4 The project is behind schedule.
5 Everything is on schedule.

B

a It's because a lot of staff have been sick.
b A day before the deadline, in fact.
c I think we'll be finished three weeks early.
d It was scheduled for 10 and we started at 10.
e I'm sure we can deliver on the date we promised.

7 Use some of the time expressions and tell your partner about your current work / projects, as in the example.

I have to do the sales figures in time for our weekly meeting on Wednesday.

KEY WORDS

deadline evaluate record review steps ahead of schedule behind schedule on schedule in time on time

FOCUS ON GRAMMAR: The passive

1 Read the email, and answer these questions with a partner.

1 Why has Igor changed his email contact address?
2 Do you receive a lot of spam or other unwanted email? What do you do with it?
3 Would you be interested in Spam-biters? Why? What other information would you like?

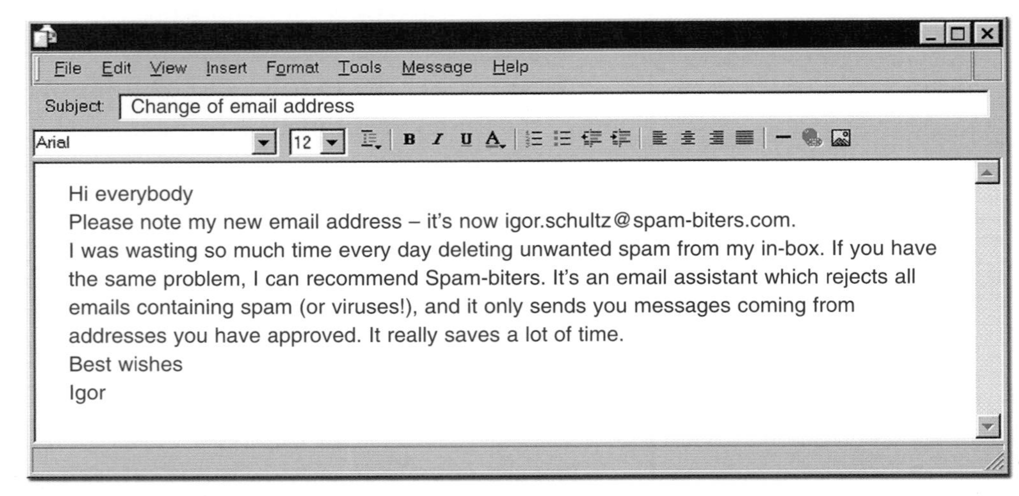

File Edit View Insert Format Tools Message Help

Subject: Change of email address

Hi everybody
Please note my new email address – it's now igor.schultz@spam-biters.com.
I was wasting so much time every day deleting unwanted spam from my in-box. If you have the same problem, I can recommend Spam-biters. It's an email assistant which rejects all emails containing spam (or viruses!), and it only sends you messages coming from addresses you have approved. It really saves a lot of time.
Best wishes
Igor

spam: email advertising or junk mail
reject: refuse
approved: accepted

2 10.2 One of the people who received Igor's email wants to know more about Spam-biters. Listen to him explaining, and complete this chart with the information in the box.

add addresses	approved contacts	checks 'contact list'
checks for viruses	rejected messages	blocked emails

Message arrives at your Spam-biters address

1 ....

Reviews 'reject list'

2 ....

Sends you messages from your 3 ....

Transfers 4 .... **to 'Blocked email log'**

Sends you regular lists of 5 ....

You 6 .... **on log to 'contact list' or 'reject list'**

3 (((10.2))) Listen to the first part again and complete these sentences.

1 First of all, the messages .... for viruses.

2 When this ...., the reject list .... to see if the sender's address is there.

KEY GRAMMAR

We form the passive with the verb *to be* and the past participle of the main verb.

*English **is spoken** all over the world.*

*I'm afraid those seats **are taken**.*

We often use the passive for describing processes, when we are more interested in the process than the person or thing doing it.

*The products **are packed** in boxes. Then, each box **is given** a barcode ...*

For more on the passive, see Language reference page 112.

4 (((10.2))) Here are some more sentences from the listening in **3**. Complete them with the passive form of the verb in brackets, then listen to check your answers.

1 After that, the same thing (do) .... for the 'contact list'.

2 If the address of the sender (include) .... in your list of approved contacts, the message (send) .... directly to you.

3 All the other messages (transfer) .... to the 'Blocked email log'.

4 Once their addresses (place) .... in your 'reject list', every new message from them (reject) ....

5 Now look at the stages of the process of producing a newspaper.

1 Put the stages in order.

2 Describe the process with a partner using the passive form, as in the examples.

First of all the stories are researched by the reporters.

When this is done, the articles are written (by the reporters).

.... Production Department prints the different pages of the newspaper.

.... Reporters email articles to Editor.

.... The company sends newspapers to different towns.

...1... Reporters research stories.

.... Sub-editor sends articles to Design Department.

.... Design Department puts articles on page and adds photos.

.... Newsagents sell newspapers to the public.

.... Sub-editor checks articles for spelling and other errors.

.... Editor checks content of articles.

...2... Reporters write articles.

FOCUS ON EXPRESSIONS 1: Managing your workload

1 How does your company monitor the progress of your work or of special projects?

2 10.3 Two managers are discussing work in progress on a customer order. Listen and complete the project status report, as in the example.

PROJECT STATUS REPORT	CUSTOMER: SNT
PRODUCT: Robot Model E243	WEEK: 12 DAY: 3

TASK	WHEN	NOTES
Final quality tests before delivery	*yesterday*	*Worked perfectly – no problems*
Training day for SNT operators	12 June	Already cancelled twice because [1] .... Now urgent, because SNT [2] ....
Installation of robot at SNT	[3]	Team of [4] .... Need to find [5] ....
Final software tests on SNT server	by end of week	[6] .... done last week: one or two [7] ....

3 10.3 Match 1–8 with a–h to make eight complete sentences. Then listen to the conversation again and check your answers.

1	Where are we ...	a	care of it.
2	We're running ...	b	out of time.
3	We need ...	c	with me.
4	I'll take ...	d	to get a move on.
5	I'm rather ...	e	to test it?
6	Leave it ...	f	on the final quality tests?
7	Have you had a chance ...	g	deal with that?
8	Can you ...	h	tied up.

4 Work with a partner. Student A, turn to File 18 page 91. Student B, turn to File 19 on page 100.

KEY EXPRESSIONS

Checking progress: *Where are we on ...? Have you had a chance to ...?*

Saying something is urgent: *We're running out of time. We need to get a move on.*

Deciding who will do what: *I'll take care of / deal with that. Leave it with me. I'm rather tied up / busy. Can you deal with that?*

FOCUS ON EXPRESSIONS 2: Saying goodbye

1 Look at these people saying goodbye. What could they say to be more polite?

2 10.4 Listen to two conversations where people are saying goodbye. What have the people been doing?

3 10.4 Listen to the two conversations again and complete these sentences.

1 Thanks ....
2 It's been .... talk to you.
3 Have a ....
4 Speak to ....
5 Thank you ....
6 It's been ....
7 I really ....

4 Work with a partner. Prepare speeches to say goodbye in different situations. Student A, turn to File 16 on page 90. Student B, turn to File 15 on page 98.

5 10.5 Listen to some sentences. Choose a response 1–8 for each sentence you hear.

1 You're very welcome. ....
2 Thanks. And you. ....
3 That's a pity. So soon? ....
4 That's OK. Any time. ....
5 Yes, it has. I'm glad you enjoyed it. ....
6 Yes. See you. ....
7 Me too. ....
8 I hope so too. ....

6 Work with a partner. Student A, turn to File 17 on page 90. Student B, turn to File 16 on page 98.

KEY EXPRESSIONS

Preparing to leave / finish, etc.: *Is that the time?* *I really must go.*

Thanking: *Thank you for inviting me.* *Thanks for everything.* *That's really helped me a lot.* *I really enjoyed it.*

Goodbye wishes: *Have a good weekend.* *See you soon.*

FOCUS ON COMMUNICATION

1 Your boss has decided to give you an assistant to help you for three hours a day.

1 What parts of your present job would you like to give to another person? Look at the cartoon below, and prepare answers to your assistant's questions.

2 Work with a partner. Take it in turns to be the new assistant. Tell the new assistant about the job, answering the questions in **1**. If you are the assistant, ask more questions if you don't understand.

3 You have your new assistant. How are you going to use the three hours a day?

2 Read the email. Underline the expressions Erik uses to thank Tamsin.

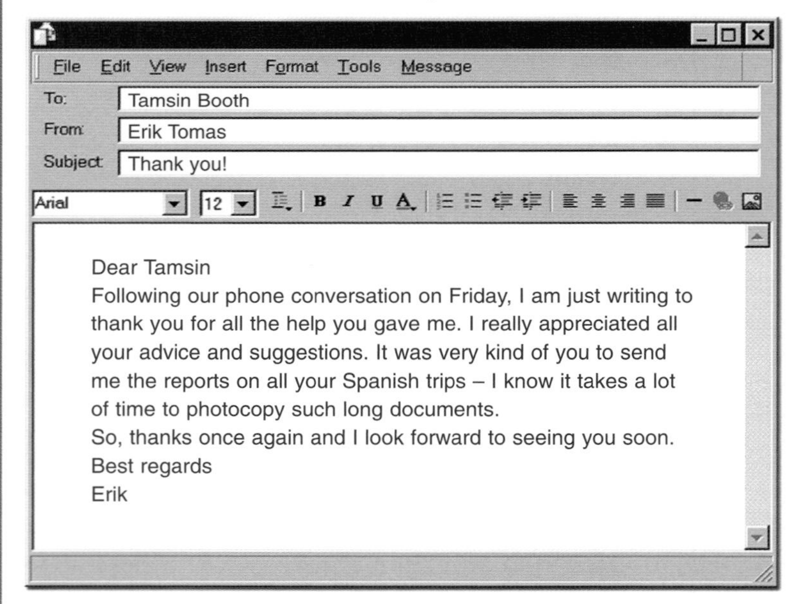

File Edit View Insert Format Tools Message

To: Tamsin Booth
From: Erik Tomas
Subject: Thank you!

Dear Tamsin
Following our phone conversation on Friday, I am just writing to thank you for all the help you gave me. I really appreciated all your advice and suggestions. It was very kind of you to send me the reports on all your Spanish trips – I know it takes a lot of time to photocopy such long documents.
So, thanks once again and I look forward to seeing you soon.
Best regards
Erik

3 You have just returned from a one-week visit to a customer in the UK. Your host, Hunter Wilson, showed you round the company and invited you for dinner at his home. He also took you to the airport early in the morning for a 6 a.m. flight. Write an email to thank him, using the expressions you underlined in **2**.

FOCUS ON BUSINESS ISSUES: Work-life balance

SPEED-DATING – *the new way to find a partner*

With the pressures of modern life, it is becoming more and more difficult for working people to find a partner. This is the philosophy behind speed-dating, a new service for single people which is all the rage in America, and has now moved to Europe.

1 Read the text and answer these questions.

1 How do you think speed-dating works?
2 Why do you think it is more difficult nowadays to find a partner?

2 10.6 Tom de Souza has been to a number of speed-dating events. Listen to an interview with him and complete the information.

Places where events happen: ....
Age groups: ....
Number of people per event: ....
Number of people you speak to: ....
Length of each conversation: ....
Subjects not talked about: ....

3 Which of these opinions on speed-dating is nearest to your own? In groups, explain your opinions.

a I think it's a great idea. Busy working people need more and more services like that to help them manage their private lives.

b The arrival of speed-dating shows once again that we are no longer in control of our own lives. Our lives control us.

END-OF-UNIT QUIZ

This is the end of Unit 10. Try this quick quiz to make sure you have understood everything.

1 Match the verbs in A with the expressions in B.

A	B
to monitor	the success / the results of a project
to schedule	customer needs / project deadlines
to evaluate	a visit / a production process
to meet	work done / progress

2 Rewrite these sentences using the passive.
 a Factory workers assemble the product.
 b Packers pack the product carefully.
 c The Finance Department prepares the invoice and sends it to the customer.
 d The customer pays the invoice within a month.

3 Choose words from the list to complete these sentences.

 out of   of   on   with   up

 a We're running .... time.
 b We have to get a move ....
 c I'll take care .... it.
 d Can you deal .... it?
 e I'm rather tied ....

4 How would you respond to these sentences?
 a Thanks for having me.
 b It's been really wonderful.
 c Have a nice weekend.

Information files
Student A

FILE 1
Unit 1
FOCUS ON GRAMMAR
EXERCISE 5, PAGE 7
STUDENT A

You and Student B work for a recruitment agency. You each have information about a candidate.

1 Ask Student B questions to find out information about their candidate, Valeria Conti.
2 Then, answer Student B's questions about Per Jenssen.

NAME	VALERIA CONTI	PER JENSSEN
Nationality	....	Swedish
Company	....	BP
Job	....	Civil Engineer
Normal residence	....	Stockholm
Present residence	....	Saudi Arabia
Main responsibility at work	....	Refinery construction
Current project	....	Build new pipeline
Interests	....	Astronomy, chess
Languages	....	English, German, French

FILE 2
Unit 1
FOCUS ON
EXPRESSIONS 2
EX 4, PAGE 9,
STUDENT A

You are going to role-play two telephone conversations with Student B.

Conversation 1

You are the caller. You begin the conversation.

- Ask to speak to Al Tyson.
- If he's not there, leave a message. You want Al Tyson to call you.
- Give your name and number.
- Thank Student B for their help.

Conversation 2

You receive a call from Student B. Student B begins the conversation.

- Student B wants to speak to Fenella Calvi. Check the spelling of Student B's name.
- Ask Student B to wait. Then, transfer the call to Fenella Calvi.

FILE 3
Unit 1

FOCUS ON COMMUNICATION EX 1.2, PAGE 10, STUDENT A

You work for SVS. You need more information about a possible recruit, Student B. Telephone him / her and complete the file below. Start and end the telephone call in a polite and natural way. You speak first.

Name	Andrea Jutter (check spelling)
Residence	....
Date of birth	....
Present employer	....
Present position	....
Present salary	....
Email address	....
Prepared to work in other cities / countries? Yes / No	
Languages	Mother tongue ....
	Other languages ....
Available when?	....

FILE 4
Unit 1

FOCUS ON COMMUNICATION EX 1.3, PAGE 10, STUDENT A

You work for SVS and you have a job offer for Andrea Jetter (Student B), who calls you back. Answer Andrea's questions about the company using the information below. Student B will speak first.

Company File

Company	FTX
Location	Albstadt, Germany
Group	Part of Assa Abloy Group (Sweden)
Activity	Locks and other security systems. Brands include: Chubb, Yale, Vachette, Lockwood Security
Employees	Germany and the Netherlands: 1,200
Job	Assistant to Sales Director. Contacts with customers and sales staff in Germany, Switzerland, and the Netherlands
Salary	€2,900 per month
Start date	In three months' time

FILE 5
Unit 2

FOCUS ON GRAMMAR EX 3, PAGE 15, STUDENT A

Complete the missing information by asking Student B questions.

1961 The company changed its name to ....

1963 They acquired Micro-Systems Inc.

1965 They opened a manufacturing plant in ....

1968 Chester Carlson died in September.

1969 Xerox moved its head office from .... to Connecticut.

1970 Xerox opened PARC (Palo Alto Research Center) in California.

FILE 6
Unit 2

FOCUS ON EXPRESSIONS
EX 6, PAGE 16,
STUDENT A

Read this information.

> You are at a conference in Gothenburg in Sweden. You work for ECM in Bologna where you are Key Accounts Manager in the European Marketing division. You joined the company in 2002.
>
> This is your first visit to Sweden. You went to Finland on holiday last year. You do not know anybody at the conference, except your boss, Carla Bulgari. You are here for all three days of the conference.

Talk to your partner using these prompts.

- Introduce yourself.
- Where / work?
- Which division?
- How often / travel for work?
- How long / stay at conference?
- When / join?
- First visit to Sweden?
- How many people / know at conference?
- Job? Marketing?

FILE 7
Unit 3

FOCUS ON GRAMMAR
EX 6, PAGE 22,
STUDENT A

1 You are a receptionist at the hotel in Hong Kong where Student B is staying. Use this information to answer his / her questions.

Transport:	You recommend the Airport Express train service, which is quicker than a taxi and there is no problem with traffic. 23-minute journey to the airport. Costs HK$100. Six trains every hour. First train at 05.50.
Check-in:	You recommend the flight check-in service at Hong Kong railway station. This is for passengers using the Airport Express service (7 check-in desks for Cathay Pacific). Open at 5.30 a.m.
Shops at airport:	Cartier, Gucci, Hermès, Disney Store, Starbucks, etc.

2 You are looking for a luxury hotel in Spain for a future conference. Phone the Hotel Alfonso XIII in Seville and find out the following information.

Location:	Where? How far from airport / railway station? Airport shuttle bus?
Facilities:	Number of rooms? Air-conditioning in rooms? How much space for meetings? Any restaurants? Business centre with computers / fax machines, etc.? Other facilities or services?
Leaving and arriving:	Check-in and check-out times?

FILE 8
Unit 3

FOCUS ON WORDS 2
EX 4, PAGE 23,
STUDENT A

Have short conversations with your partner for these four situations.

1 You are checking out of the hotel. Student B is the receptionist.
  - Say you want to check out.
    I'd like to check out please.
  - Ask for your bill.
  - Ask if you can book a room for next month (2 nights).
  - Ask for the time of the next shuttle bus to the airport.
  - Ask if the shuttle bus goes to Terminal 2 of the airport.
2 You work in the ticket office of the train station. Student B is a passenger. Respond to his / her questions. Invent your answers.
3 You are at the departure gate. They announced your flight to Chicago thirty minutes ago, but nothing is happening. Student B is an airline employee.
  - Ask why there's a delay.
  - Ask when boarding will start.
  - Ask what time the plane will land.
  - Ask for the terminal number of your connecting flight in Chicago.
4 You are a hotel receptionist. Student B is a guest who has just arrived. Respond to his / her questions. Invent your answers.

FILE 9
Unit 4

FOCUS ON EXPRESSIONS
EX 9.2, PAGE 33,
STUDENT A

You are Philip Johnson. You receive a call from Marianne about an interview. Try to find a suitable time using your diary below.

FILE 10
Unit 5

FOCUS ON GRAMMAR
EX 4, PAGE 39,
STUDENT A

1 Look at the problems 1–5 below. Complete the gaps with the comparative form of one of these words: *cheap, detailed, big, few, reliable.*

2 Describe problems 1–5 to your partner as in the example.
Sixty-four per cent of Internet shoppers wanted ...

3 Listen to your partner's description of problems 6–10 and complete the table.

4 Have you experienced any of these problems yourself?

TOP 10 PROBLEMS EXPERIENCED BY INTERNET SHOPPERS

	PROBLEM	PERCENTAGE OF INTERNET BUYERS
1	Wanted .... stocks so items were always available.	64
2	Thought that delivery times should be	40
3	Thought that delivery costs should be	38
4	Wanted .... problems with connections.	36
5	Wanted .... information about progress of the order.	28
6	Wanted a .... of goods.	....
7	Thought it should be .... around the website.	....
8	Wanted .... about how to make a purchase.	....
9	Thought that	....
10	Wanted more and	....

FILE 11
Unit 5

FOCUS ON EXPRESSIONS
EX 8, PAGE 41,
STUDENT A

These are your views on the four proposals.

- You like option **a**. Customers will like the idea of getting free petrol.
- You also like option **c**. This will give the driver the chance to go to the shop / toilet, etc. while the employee is filling his car.
- You don't like option **b**. People don't want good food when they're travelling. They just want to eat quickly and leave.
- You're not sure about option **d**. Don't small cars have a capacity of less than 40 litres?

FILE 12
Unit 6

FOCUS ON GRAMMAR 1
EX 4, PAGE 46,
STUDENT A

You are a customer. Your partner (Student B) is one of your suppliers.

1 Phone your partner and explain the points below. Make a note of the solutions he / she offers. Start like this:
Hello. This is .... I'm calling to check a few things with you. First of all ...
- You often receive deliveries after 12 midday. This is too late.
- You don't know the supplier's latest prices.
- You now place very big orders. You'd like to renegotiate prices.
- Your computer system crashed yesterday. You've lost all the order details for this month.

2 Your partner is going to explain four problems he / she has. Choose a solution from this list, and make a decision using *I'll ...* or *We'll ...* .
- Send a complete list of names, phone numbers, and email addresses.
- Talk to the Accounts Manager.
- Ask the security guard to open the main gate at 5.30 a.m.
- Try to place orders earlier in the day.

3 Now confirm with your supplier what you have decided to do. Use *going to.*
So I'm going to talk to the Accounts Manager about the payment problem.
You're going to ...

FILE 13
Unit 6

FOCUS ON EXPRESSIONS
EX 6, PAGE 47,
STUDENT A

1 You are a sales rep. Your boss (Student B) sent you the message below. Explain to your boss why you can't do the different things (see your notes in blue on the message for reasons). Your boss will respond.
I'm afraid,I can't prepare a schedule because I don't know what day he is going to arrive.

> Could you do these things for me today?
> – prepare a provisional schedule for the CEO's visit next week *Arrival date?*
> – book me a British Airways flight to Timbuktu *BA don't fly there.*
> – phone Lisa Martell at AFK to cancel my meeting tomorrow *Don't have her number.*
> – order 2 giant pizzas from Fat Sam's for today's lunchtime meeting. *Restaurant is closed.*

2 You are a manager. You sent the message below to your Personal Assistant (Student B). He / she can't do the different things. Listen to his / her explanations, then respond appropriately, suggesting an alternative.

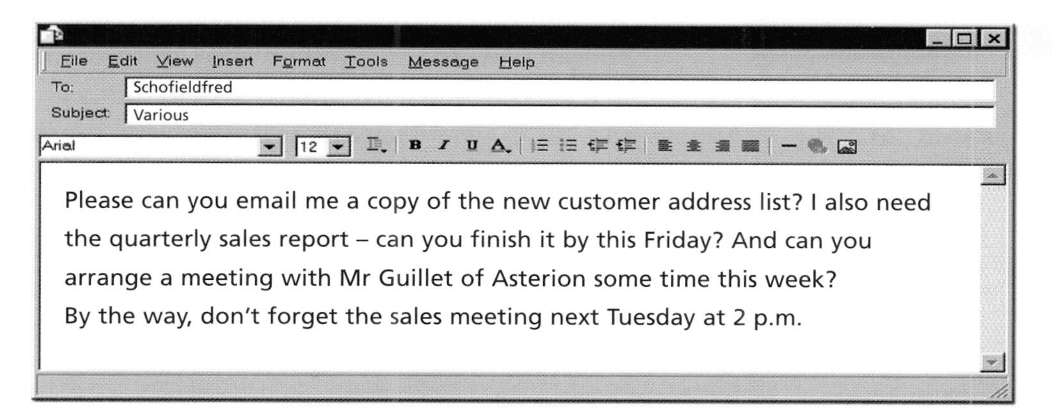
File Edit View Insert Format Tools Message Help
To: Schofieldfred
Subject: Various

Please can you email me a copy of the new customer address list? I also need the quarterly sales report – can you finish it by this Friday? And can you arrange a meeting with Mr Guillet of Asterion some time this week?
By the way, don't forget the sales meeting next Tuesday at 2 p.m.

FILE 14
Unit 7

FOCUS ON EXPRESSIONS
EX 7, PAGE 57,
STUDENT A

Look at the information on this slide and present it to your partner.

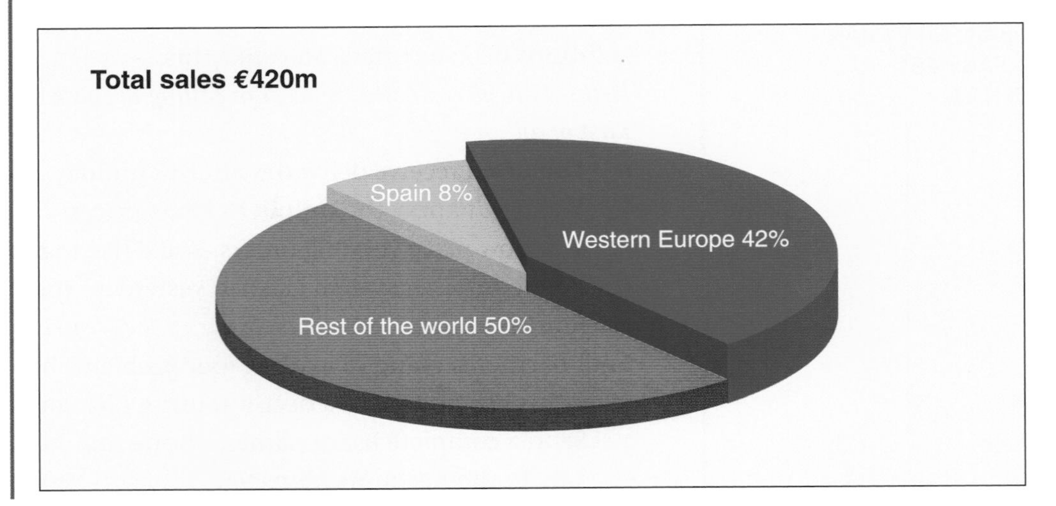

FILE 15
Unit 9

FOCUS ON
EXPRESSIONS 2
EX 3, PAGE 73,
STUDENT A

You are chairing the meeting. Control the discussion and make sure that everybody follows the agenda.

- Each person has to present the sales results for their country and say what money they want to spend on advertising this year. Take notes and ask for more information where necessary.
- As Advertising Manager for Central Europe you are responsible for budgets. Last year was expensive (€35m), and you mustn't spend much more this year.
- If you are in a group of three you should also present the information for the Czech Republic, as the Sales Manager of this country isn't here today. Turn to File 4 on page 102.

FILE 16
Unit 10

FOCUS ON
EXPRESSIONS 2
EX 4, PAGE 81,
STUDENT A

Prepare a speech for this situation. Give the speech and ask your partner what he / she thinks the situation was.

> As Sales Director, you have to say a few words to close your company's annual sales conference. You've learnt a lot about the different sales regions. The sales managers are going back to their different countries, but you plan to visit many of them in the next few months.

FILE 17
Unit 10

FOCUS ON
EXPRESSIONS 2
EX 6, PAGE 81,
STUDENT A

You and your partner (Student B) have been at a three-day business conference in Kansas, USA. You have just finished lunch: Student B paid for your food. It is time to leave the conference and go back to your own country. Respond appropriately to what Student B says: try to use the expressions on page 81.
You start the conversation.

- Thank Student B for the food.
- Invite Student B to have dinner with you next time you meet. You will pay.
- You hope to see Student B in two weeks at the Munich Trade Fair.
- Say goodbye.

FILE 18
Unit 10

FOCUS ON EXPRESSIONS 1 EX 4, PAGE 80, STUDENT A

You and your partner are colleagues in the sales department of a manufacturing company. You were both going on a sales trip to Spain in three days. This has been cancelled, and you have now been asked to visit a new client in Germany, Mr Fessenmayer.

1 You are responsible for the travel arrangements. Your partner will ask you about progress on this. Answer with reference to the handwritten notes. If a task isn't done, decide who's going to deal with it.
2 Then ask your partner about the business arrangements and make notes on the answers.
   Where are we on the meeting in Munich? Have you had a chance to email ...?

Travel arrangements

1 Call travel agent to arrange flights to Munich	Done – leaving 17th at 17.45.
2 Send air tickets for Spain back to travel agent	Not done, but will do when less busy!
3 Book two hotel rooms in Munich	Done – staying at Königshotel on 16th/17th.
4 Cancel reservation for Hotel Altamira, Madrid	Not done – receptionist doesn't speak English and email address doesn't work. Ask your colleague – he/she speaks Spanish!
5 Reserve a rental car from Munich airport	Have tried, but nothing available. But doesn't your partner know someone in the car rental business?

Business arrangements

1 Email Mr Fessenmayer to confirm meeting.
2 Prepare slides for presentation.
3 Send copy of brochure to Mr Fessenmayer.
4 Ask Production Manager for product samples.
5 Buy birthday present for wife/husband/partner.

Information files
Student B

FILE 1
Unit 1

FOCUS ON GRAMMAR
EX 5, PAGE 7,
STUDENT B

You and Student A work for a recruitment agency. You each have information about a candidate.

1 Answer Student A's questions about Valeria Conti.
2 Then, ask Student A questions to find out information about their candidate, Per Jenssen.

NAME	VALERIA CONTI	PER JENSSEN
Nationality	Italian	....
Company	Unilever	....
Job	Laundry Scientist	....
Permanent residence	Rome	....
Present residence	New Jersey	....
Main responsibility at work	Tests washing products	....
Current project	New tablet detergent	....
Interests	Tennis, theatre	....
Languages	English	....

FILE 2
Unit 1

FOCUS ON
EXPRESSIONS 2
EX 4, PAGE 9,
STUDENT B

You are going to role-play two telephone conversations with Student A.

Conversation 1

You receive a call from Student A. Student A begins the conversation.

- Student A wants to speak to Al Tyson. He is in a meeting. Offer to take a message.
- Check Student A's name and telephone number.
- Say you will give Al Tyson the message.

Conversation 2

You are the caller. You begin the conversation.

- Say who you are and where you are calling from. Ask to speak to Fenella Calvi.
- Spell your name.

FILE 3
Unit 1

FOCUS ON COMMUNICATION EX 1.2, PAGE 10, STUDENT B

Your name is Andrea Jetter. You are looking for a new job. Student A from SVS telephones you for more information. Answer the telephone and give the information. Student A will speak first.

Name	Andrea Jetter
Residence	Stuttgart
Date of birth	31.05.78
Present employer	ZJI GmbH
Present position	Assistant to Financial Director
Present salary	€2,500 per month
Email address	Jetter@ZJI.com
Prepared to work in other cities / countries?	Austria or Netherlands
Languages:	
Mother tongue	German
Other languages	English and Dutch
Available when?	Two months' notice to present employer

FILE 4
Unit 1

FOCUS ON COMMUNICATION EX 1.3, PAGE 10, STUDENT B

You are Andrea Jetter. You got the message from SVS. Call back and ask for the following information. Start and end the conversation in a polite and natural way. You speak first.

1 Explain why you are calling.
2 Ask about the company:
   - Name?
   - Location?
   - Part of a group? Any famous brands?
   - Size of company?
3 Ask about the job:
   - Salary?
   - Start date?
4 Tell Student A you would like some time to think about the job.
5 End the call politely.

FILE 5
Unit 2

FOCUS ON GRAMMAR EX 3, PAGE 15, STUDENT B

Complete the missing information by asking Student A questions.

1961 The company changed its name to Xerox Corporation.
.... They acquired Micro-Systems Inc.
1965 They opened a manufacturing plant in Venray, the Netherlands.
1968 Chester Carlson died in ....
1969 Xerox moved its head office from New York to Connecticut.
1970 Xerox opened .... in California.

FILE 6
Unit 2

FOCUS ON EXPRESSIONS
EX 6, PAGE 16,
STUDENT B

Read this information.

You are at a conference in Gothenburg in Sweden. You work in the European Marketing division of ECM in Barcelona, where you are Regional Sales Director for Eastern Spain. You joined the company in 1998.

You travel in Europe about three or four times a year. This is your second visit to Sweden. You came here in 2001 for a product launch.

You know a lot of people at the conference, and you are a good friend of Carla Bulgari. You are here for the first two days of the conference.

Talk to your partner using the following prompts.

- Introduce yourself.
- Where / work?
- Which division?
- Job? Marketing?
- When / join?
- First visit to Sweden?
- How many people / know at conference?
- How long / stay at conference?
- Offer to introduce him / her to some other people.

FILE 7
Unit 3

FOCUS ON GRAMMAR
EX 6, PAGE 22,
STUDENT B

1 You are staying at a hotel near Hong Kong station. You have a flight home from Chek Lap Kok Airport tomorrow morning at 10.30 a.m. Find out the following information.

Transport:	Best way to get to airport? Time needed to get there? Cost? Number of trains per hour? First train in morning?
Check-in:	Where? Check-in desks for Cathay Pacific? Opening time of check-in desks?
Shopping:	Presents for your family – any good shops at airport?

2 You are a receptionist at the Hotel Alfonso XIII in Seville in Spain. Student A will call you to ask for information. Use this information to answer his / her questions.

Location:	In centre of Seville, 3 km from railway station, 14 km from Seville airport (shuttle bus from hotel available)
Facilities include:	146 rooms (all air-conditioned with cable TV)
	7 meeting rooms
	2 restaurants on site. One serves local specialities, the other Japanese.
	Outdoor swimming pool
	Free car park
	Shops
	Bar
Other business facilities:	Business centre
Leaving and arriving:	Check-out before midday, check-in after 2 p.m.

FILE 8
Unit 3

FOCUS ON WORDS 2
EX 4, PAGE 23,
STUDENT B

Have short conversations with your partner for these four situations.

1 You are a hotel receptionist. Student A is a guest. Respond to his / her questions. Invent your answers.
2 You are a passenger at the train station. Student A works in the ticket office.
   - Ask for the time of the next train to city centre.

   What time does the next train for the city centre leave?
   - Ask about one-way and return fares.
   - Ask for a one-way ticket.
   - Ask for a timetable.
   - Ask about the platform.
3 You are an airline employee at the departure gate. There's a delay in boarding. Student A is a passenger. Respond to his / her questions. Invent your answers.
4 You are arriving at a hotel and you want a room. Student A is the hotel receptionist.
   - Ask if they have a single room for one night.
   - Ask if there's a car park.
   - Ask if there's a safe for your valuables.
   - Ask about the check-out time.

FILE 9
Unit 4

FOCUS ON EXPRESSIONS
EX 9.1, PAGE 33,
STUDENT B

You are Emilie Thomas. You receive a call from Marianne about an interview. Try to find a suitable time using your diary below.

Week 23 — June	Week 24 — June
7th Monday *Holiday until Wednesday*	*14th Monday* *8.30 Car - garage* *2.00 Dentist*
8th Tuesday	*15th Tuesday*
9th Wednesday	*16th Wednesday* *10.00-5.30 Sales training Manchester*
10th Thursday *10.00-1.00 Monthly finance meeting*	*17th Thursday* *Trade fair Newcastle*
11th Friday *10.00-4.00 Interviews for new reps*	*18th Friday* *9.30-4.30 Regional sales meeting Birmingham*

FILE 10
Unit 5

FOCUS ON GRAMMAR
EX 4, PAGE 39,
STUDENT B

1 Look at the problems 6–10 below. Complete the gaps with the comparative form of one of these words: *competitive, good, wide, easy, clear.*
2 Listen to your partner's description of problems 1–5 and complete the table.
3 Describe problems 6–10 to your partner, as in the example.
Twenty-seven per cent of Internet shoppers wanted ...
4 Have you experienced any of these problems yourself?

TOP 10 PROBLEMS EXPERIENCED BY INTERNET SHOPPERS

	PROBLEM	PERCENTAGE OF INTERNET BUYERS
1	Wanted .... so items were always available.	....
2	Thought that .... should be	....
3	Thought that .... should be	....
4	Wanted .... with connections.	....
5	Wanted .... about progress of the order.	....
6	Wanted a .... selection of goods.	27
7	Thought it should be .... to find their way around the website.	26
8	Wanted .... information about how to make a purchase.	25
9	Thought that prices should be	22
10	Wanted more and .... ideas for gifts.	16

FILE 11
Unit 6

FOCUS ON GRAMMAR 1
EX 4, PAGE 46,
STUDENT B

You are a supplier. Your partner (Student A) is one of your customers.

1 Your partner is going to phone you to explain four problems he / she has. Choose a solution from this list, and make a decision using *I'll ...* or *We'll ...* .
- Ask the Sales Manager to phone your customer.
- Email a list of orders and deliveries for the last four weeks.
- Arrange all deliveries for the morning.
- Send the new brochure and price list.

2 When your partner has finished, explain the points below. Make a note of the solutions he / she offers. Introduce the subject like this:
Before you go, I also have one or two things to ask you. First of all, ...
- Payment for the last three invoices has been a month late. Is there a problem?
- If your customer wants next-day delivery, please can he / she order before 2 p.m.?
- You'd like to have the contact details of all your customer's warehouse managers.
- Your drivers sometimes want to deliver before 7 a.m., but the entrance to your customer's central warehouse is always closed.

3 Now confirm with your supplier what you have decided to do. Use *going to.*
So I'm going to ask the Sales Manager to phone you. You're going to ...

FILE 12
Unit 5

FOCUS ON EXPRESSIONS
EX 8, PAGE 41,
STUDENT B

These are your views on the four proposals:

- You like option **b**. PEO has an image of good quality; improving the food will help this image.
- You also like option **d**. cars get very dirty on motorways, so customers will love this service.
- You don't like option **a**. Many of PEO's competitors have loyalty cards, so it's not a new idea.
- You're not sure about option **c**. Is it necessary to employ extra staff? Can't the present staff do the job?

FILE 13
Unit 6

FOCUS ON EXPRESSIONS
EX 6, PAGE 47,
STUDENT B

1 You are a Sales Manager. You sent the message below to one of your sales reps (Student A). He / she can't do the different things. Listen to his / her explanations, then respond, suggesting an alternative,
Oh dear. That's a pity. Can you contact him and ask him?

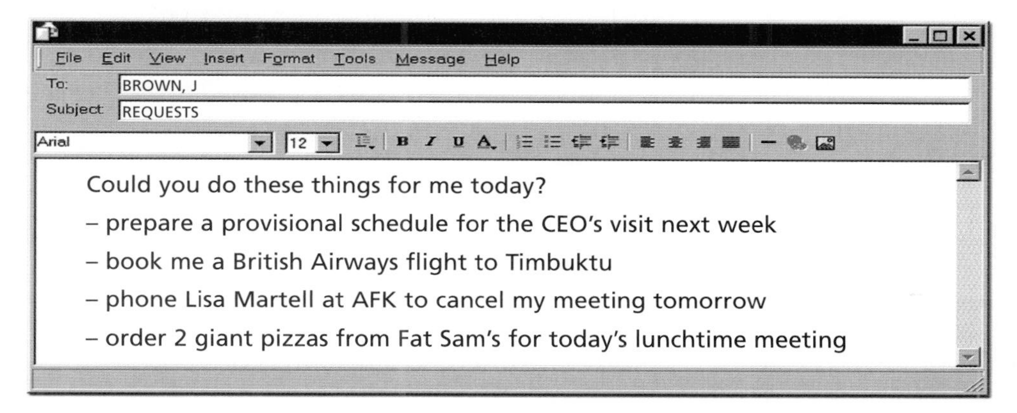

2 You are a sales rep. Your boss (Student A) sent you the message below. Explain to your boss why you can't do the different things (see your notes in blue on the message for reasons). Your boss will respond.
I'm afraid I can't email you the address list because it's incomplete.

Please can you email me a copy of the new customer address list? *List is incomplete.*
I also need the quarterly sales report – can you finish it by this Friday? *On a business trip on Wednesday and Thursday.*
And can you arrange a meeting with Mr Guillet of Asterion some time this week? *Don't have contact details.*
PS Don't forget the sales meeting next Tuesday at 2 p.m. *Don't have all sales figures yet.*

FILE 14
Unit 7

FOCUS ON EXPRESSIONS
EX 7, PAGE 57,
STUDENT B

Look at the information on this slide and present it to your partner.

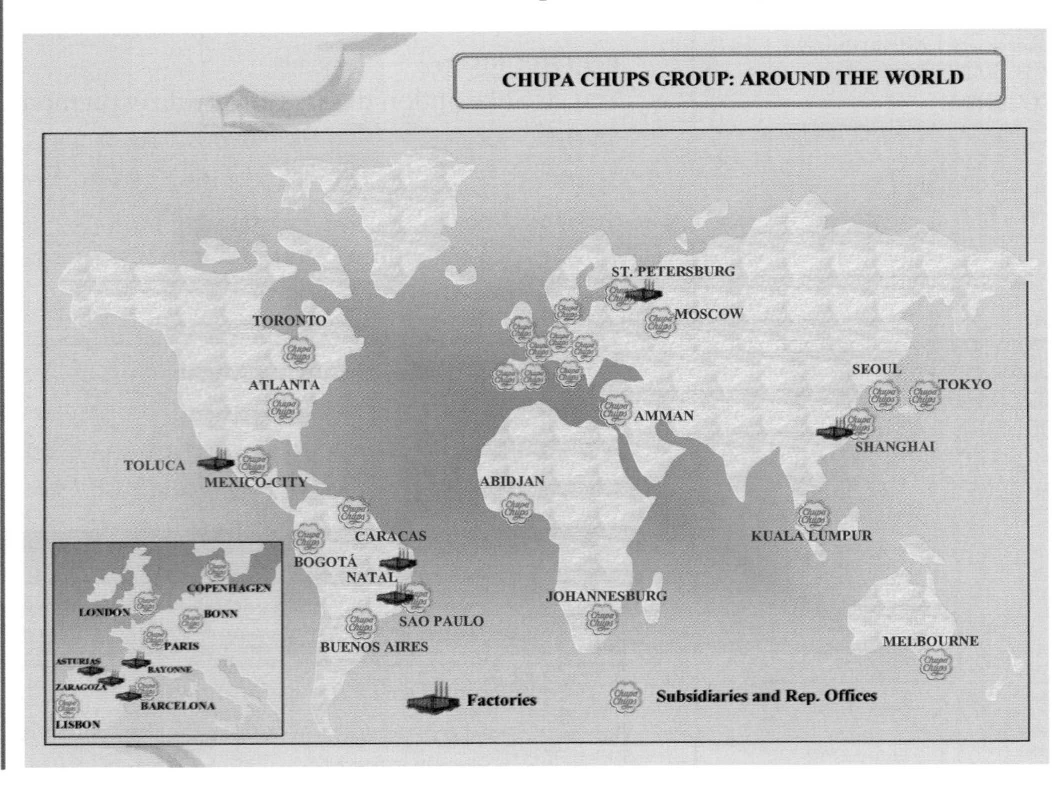

FILE 15
Unit 10

FOCUS ON
EXPRESSIONS 2
EX 4, PAGE 81,
STUDENT B

Prepare a speech for this situation. Give the speech and ask your partner what he / she thinks the situation was.

> It's Friday evening. The eighty-year-old ex-president of your company has just finished his annual speech to the staff. As usual, it was much too long, and everybody wants to go home. Say a few words to the ex-president and the staff.

FILE 16
Unit 10

FOCUS ON
EXPRESSIONS 2
EX 6, PAGE 81,
STUDENT B

You and your partner (Student A) have been at a three-day business conference in Kansas, USA. You have just finished lunch: you paid for the food. It is time to leave the conference and go back to your own country. Respond appropriately to what Student A says: try to use the expressions on page 81.
Student A starts the conversation.

- Student A has given you some useful information about the South American market. Say thank you.
- You thought the conference was excellent.
- You have to catch a plane in two hours.
- Say goodbye.

FILE 17
Unit 8

FOCUS ON COMMUNICATION EX 1, PAGE 66, STUDENT B

Next week you are visiting a foreign supplier, Student A. You are arriving at 4 p.m. and leaving at the same time the next day. Student A will phone you to arrange your accommodation and plan your schedule.

1 Use the information below to respond to his / her questions.
2 Then ask questions of your own to find out what the possibilities are.
What kind of food do they serve?
If we don't (play golf), will we have time to (go shopping)?
I'm afraid I'm not very keen on ... . Perhaps we could ... instead?

You're fond of:
- modern hotels
- nice long lunches
- good wine
- French food (but you're vegetarian)
- classical music
- golf (but you have a bad leg at the moment)
- tennis (your favourite sport)
- shopping for presents for your family.

You aren't keen on:
- hotels in the centre of town (too noisy)
- pizza and pasta
- visiting old buildings (you prefer modern architecture).

FILE 18
Unit 9

FOCUS ON EXPRESSIONS 2 EX 3, PAGE 73, STUDENT B

You are the Sales Manager for Poland. Listen to your colleagues from other countries and take notes, asking for more information where necessary.
The Advertising Manager will ask you to present these sales results for last year.

- 1st quarter: €22.5m
- 2nd quarter: €31.2m
- 3rd quarter: €35.7m
- 4th quarter: €37.1m

Remarks: The outdoor advertising campaign in the first half of the year was very successful. The rise in sales was slower at the end of the year because of new competition. You must do something about this.

Needs: You must have €25-30m this year for a TV advertising campaign.
You also need some new furniture for your office in Poland!

FILE 19
Unit 10

FOCUS ON EXPRESSIONS 1
EX 4, PAGE 80,
STUDENT B

You and your partner are colleagues in the Sales Department of a manufacturing company. You were both going on a sales trip to Spain in three days. This has been cancelled, and you have now been asked to visit a new client in Germany, Mr Fessenmayer.

1 Your partner is responsible for the travel arrangements.
Ask him / her about progress on this and make notes on the answers.
Where are we on the flights to Munich? Have you had a chance to call ...?
2 Then your partner will ask you about the business arrangements. Answer with reference to the handwritten notes. If a task isn't done, decide who's going to deal with it.

Travel arrangements

1 Call travel agent to arrange flights to Munich
2 Send air tickets for Spain back to travel agent
3 Book two hotel rooms in Munich
4 Cancel reservation for Hotel Altamira, Madrid
5 Reserve a rental car from Munich airport

Business arrangements

1 Email Mr Fessenmayer to confirm meeting	Done. Meeting confirmed for 17th at 10.30 a.m.
2 Prepare slides for presentation	Not done, but will do - quite urgent now.
3 Send copy of brochure to Mr Fessenmayer	Not done - don't have his full postal address. Maybe your partner has it?
4 Ask Production Manager for product samples	Not done- he's not here today or tomorrow.
5 Buy birthday present for wife/husband/partner.	Not done - no time. Birthday is tomorrow!

Extra information files

FILE 1
Unit 5
FOCUS ON EXPRESSIONS
EX 8, PAGE 41,
STUDENT C

These are your views on the four proposals:
- You like option **b**. Your competitors have very bad food in their cafés.
- You also like option **c**. This idea works very well in the USA.
- You don't like option **d**. People wash their car before or after a long trip, not during the trip.
- You're not sure about option **a**. Isn't it better to give free gifts, not free petrol?

FILE 2
Unit 9
FOCUS ON
EXPRESSIONS 2
EX 3, PAGE 73,
STUDENT C

You are the Sales Manager for Hungary. Listen to your colleagues from other countries and take notes, asking for more information where necessary.
The Advertising Manager will ask you to present these sales results for last year.

- 1st quarter: €16.3m
- 2nd quarter: €17.5m
- 3rd quarter: €16.9m
- 4th quarter: €28.4m

Remarks: The first nine months were difficult because of logistical problems. The point-of-sale advertising campaign in the first three months of the year didn't work very well. You did more outdoor advertising in the third quarter, and results were much better after that.

Needs: You must have €20–25m this year for a new outdoor advertising campaign. You also want to know why the advertising budget for Asia is much higher than for Central Europe.

FILE 3
Unit 5

FOCUS ON EXPRESSIONS
EX 8, PAGE 41,
STUDENT D

These are your views on the four proposals:

- You like option **a**. None of your competitors offers free petrol.
- You also like option **d**. Even at half price, PEO will make a profit on the car wash.
- You don't like option **c**. People prefer to serve themselves at petrol stations.
- You're not sure about option **b**. Why not improve the food, but make customers pay more?

FILE 4
Unit 9

FOCUS ON
EXPRESSIONS 2
EX 3, PAGE 73,
STUDENT D

You are the Sales Manager for the Czech Republic. Listen to your colleagues from other countries and take notes, asking for more information where necessary. The Advertising Manager will ask you to present these sales results for last year.

- 1st quarter: €11.6m
- 2nd quarter: €12.8m
- 3rd quarter: €12.6m
- 4th quarter: €15.7m

Remarks: Your budget for advertising last year was much too low. Sales were better at the end of the year because of the 'Christmas effect', but this won't continue; not enough people know the Fitstart brand.

Needs: You must have €15-20m this year for a new advertising campaign on local radio, and in newspapers and magazines. You also want to know why Poland always receives more money for advertising than the Czech Republic or Hungary!

FILE 5
Unit 9

FOCUS ON
COMMUNICATION
EX 1.2, PAGE 74,
STUDENTS A AND B

Here is some more information about trends in publishing.

1 Look at the information in the graphs and tables and describe the trends.
2 Turn back to 1 on page 74 and decide how important the trends are.

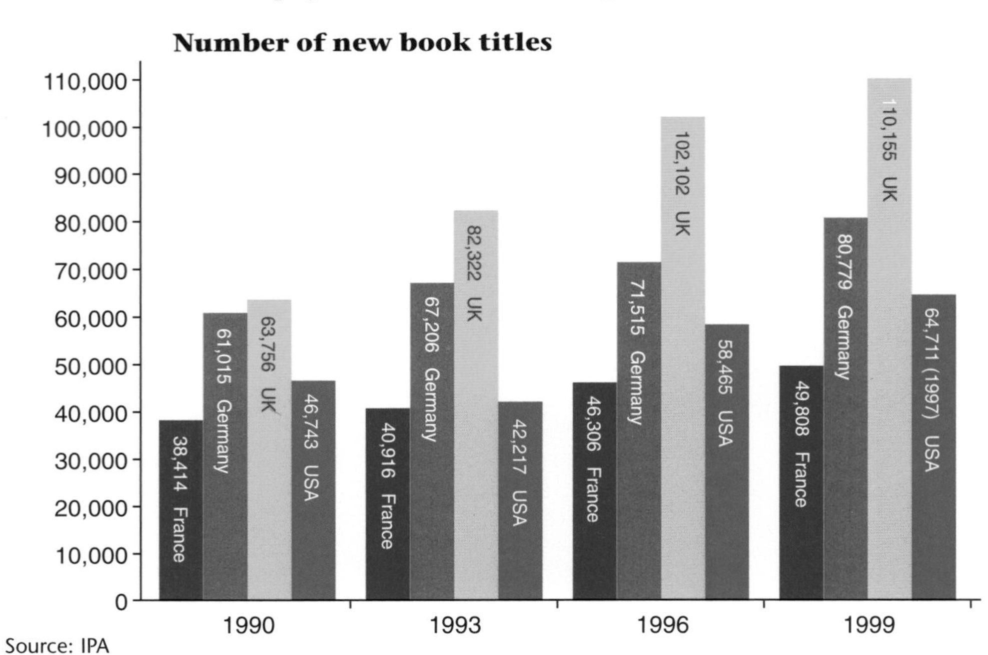

Source: IPA

SPENDING ON BOOKS		
Country	$ per person per year (2000)	$ per person per year (2002)
France	50	47
Germany	109	120
UK	79	78
USA	90	98

Source: Economist World in Figures 2002

ESTIMATED NUMBER OF INTERNET USERS			
Country	Population (m)	% of population with Internet (1998)	% of population with Internet (2001)
France	58.5	5.2[1]	19.65[3]
Germany	82.1	7.3[1]	34.49[2]
UK	58.5	9.0[1]	55.32[4]
USA	271.8	23.0[5]	59.75[2]

Sources: NOP Research group (1), Nielsen Net Ratings (2),
Sessi (3), Jupiter MMXI (4), Intelliquest (5)

Magazine adspend in US$ million

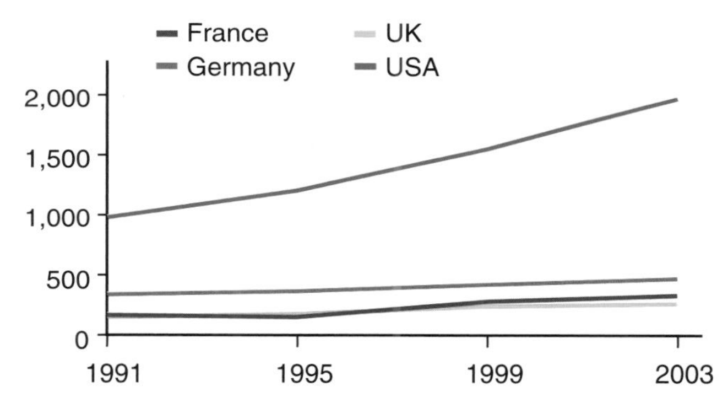

Source: www.fipp.com

% of total adspend for magazines

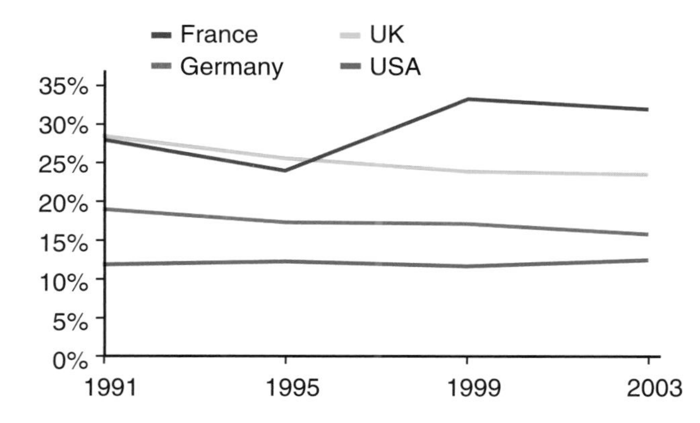

Source: www.fipp.com

Language reference

GRAMMAR

USEFUL LANGUAGE AND EXPRESSIONS

GRAMMAR

1 ADJECTIVES AND ADVERBS

1 We usually place adjectives before the noun.
*He's a **good** salesman.*
*She's a very **helpful** colleague.*

2 We usually place adverbs after the verb.
*Could you work **quietly** please? I'm trying to concentrate.*
*He writes **carefully**.*

3 Form: We usually add *-ly* to the adjective to form an adverb.
*She's a **quick** worker. She works **quickly**.*

4 Some adverbs are irregular.
good → *well*   *fast* → *fast*

5 Adverbs of frequency, such as *often*, *sometimes*, *never*, *rarely*, and *always*, are usually placed before the main verb.
*I **often** travel abroad on business.*
*She **never** speaks at meetings.*

6 Adverbs of frequency are placed after *be*, an auxiliary verb, or a modal verb.
*He is **usually** late.*
*I have **never** been to Berlin.*
*I can't **always** find a parking space.*

COMMON ERRORS

~~*She works often late.*~~ → *She often works late.*
~~*He is a boss very difficult.*~~ → *He is a very difficult boss.*
~~*They speak French good.*~~ → *They speak French well.*

CHECK YOUR UNDERSTANDING

Put these sentences in the correct order.

1 work They as team effectively a.
2 difficult It's project a to very do.
3 arrives late at often She work.
4 fast He is very learner a.
5 learns He fast.
6 rarely office in She before is her nine o'clock.
7 I usually Saturday on work don't a.

2 ARTICLES

1 We use *a* before a singular countable noun or adjective + noun combination.
*I work in **a** bank.*
*They live in **a** nice house.*

2 When the noun or adjective begins with a vowel or a vowel sound, we use *an*.
*I need **an** envelope.*
*It takes me **an** hour to get to work.*

3 We use *a* / *an* when we do not need to say which particular thing we are talking about.
*I work in **an** office.*

4. We use *the* before countable and uncountable nouns to say which particular thing we are talking about, or when only one exists.
__The__ bank is near __the__ city centre.
She likes __the__ flowers that we bought her.

5. When we talk about named rivers and seas we use *the*.
__the__ Danube, __the__ Mediterranean

6. When we talk about plural place names we use *the*.
__the__ USA, __the__ UAE

7. When we say what our job is, we use *a* or *an*.
I am __a__ pilot.

8. We do not use an article before plural or uncountable nouns when we are talking about things in general.
She likes flowers.

9. We do not use an article before languages, most streets, cities, and countries.
Only a few people in our company speak Spanish.
The journey from England to Australia is very long.

10. We do not use an article before names of mountains, lakes, airports, and stations.
They climbed Mount Everest.
I need to go to Narita airport.

COMMON ERRORS

~~Is there the bank near here?~~ → *Is there a bank near here?*
~~I am doctor.~~ → *I am a doctor.*
~~Next year we are going to the Spain.~~ → *Next year we are going to Spain.*
~~Do you speak the English?~~ → *Do you speak English?*

CHECK YOUR UNDERSTANDING

Complete these sentences with *a*, *an*, *the*, or no article (Ø).

1. She is .... pilot with Qantas.
2. Her office is on .... third floor.
3. My apartment is in .... city centre near .... Seine.
4. Could I talk to .... person in charge of marketing?
5. I work for .... Italian company.
6. We would like to visit .... Lake Como this year.
7. Have you found .... information that I wanted?

3 COMPARATIVES AND SUPERLATIVES

Comparatives

1. We usually add *-er* to the adjective.
This machine is __quicker__ than that one.

2. With short adjectives that end in vowel (*a*, *e*, *i*, *o*, *u*) + consonant (*b*, *c*, *d*, *f*, etc.), we double the final consonant and add *-er*.
big → ***bigger***   *thin* → ***thinner***

3. For long adjectives we put *more* or *less* before the adjective.
This machine is __more economical__ than that one.
That machine is __less expensive__ than the other one.

4 Some adjectives ending in *-y* become *-ier*.
*My last job was **easier** than my present one.*

5 Some adjectives have an irregular comparative form.
good ➔ *better* *bad* ➔ *worse* *far* ➔ *further*

6 We can use *(not) as* + adjective + *as*, to say that two things are (not) the same.
*This calculator is **not as good as** that one.*

Superlatives

1 We usually add *the* + *-est* to the adjective.
*This machine is **the quickest** of all.*

2 With short adjectives that end in vowel + consonant, we double the final consonant and add *-est*.
big ➔ *the bi**ggest*** *thin* ➔ *the thi**nnest***

3 For long adjectives we put *the most* or *the least* before the adjective.
*This machine is **the most economical** on the market.*
*That machine is **the least expensive** of all.*

4 Some adjectives ending in *-y* become *-iest*.
*For me Thursday is **the easiest** day of the week.*

5 Some adjectives have an irregular superlative form.
good ➔ *the best* *bad* ➔ *the worst* *far* ➔ *the furthest*

COMMON ERRORS

~~This fax machine is not as efficient than that one.~~ ➔ *This fax machine is not as efficient as that one.*
~~This hotel is the cheap I could find.~~ ➔ *This hotel is the cheapest I could find.*

CHECK YOUR UNDERSTANDING

Complete these sentences using the comparative or superlative form of the adjective in brackets, as in the example.

1 Our Managing Director is (young) ....younger.... than the Financial Director.
2 The company was (profitable) .... last year than this year.
3 We have seven factories: the (large) .... one is in Mexico.
4 Hotels in London are (expensive) .... than in Paris.
5 I think our new brochure is (good) .... than our competitors'.
6 Our (famous) .... product is the VS520.
7 1995 was the (bad) .... year for our company ever.
8 Germany is the (large) .... country in the EU.

4 CONDITIONALS: 1ST AND 2ND CONDITIONALS

1st conditional

1 We use the 1st conditional to talk about something in the future which will probably happen in certain situations.
***If** you **leave** at 2.00, you **will be** in Washington by 9.00.*
*We **won't go** out for dinner **if** you **don't want to**.*
***If** I **have** time, **I'll visit** Kyoto.*
*They **won't eat** before the meeting **if** they **aren't** hungry.*

2 Form: *if* + present simple, *will / won't* + infinitive.

2nd conditional

1 We use the 2nd conditional to imagine what might happen in certain situations.

***If** I **earned** more, I **would eat** out more often.*

*He'**d get** the job **if** he **spoke** fluent German.*

***If** I **had** time, I'**d go** to the gym more often.*

*Travelling to work **would be** easier **if** I **had** a car.*

2 We can use the *were* form of the 2nd conditional to give or ask for advice.

***If I were you** I'd change jobs.*

*What would you do **if you were me**?*

3 Form: *if* + past simple, *would / wouldn't* + infinitive.

COMMON ERRORS

~~*If I will go, I will see you there.*~~ → *If I go, I will see you there.*

~~*If I would be the CEO, I would have an enormous office.*~~ → *If I was the CEO, I would have an enormous office.*

CHECK YOUR UNDERSTANDING

1 Match a clause from A with a clause from B to make sentences.

	A		B
1	If I were you ...	a	if you work a little harder.
2	She'll meet you at the station ...	b	they would be less busy.
3	If I finish this work by 5.00 ...	c	if you don't tell him.
4	If they employed just one more person ...	d	if you get there before 6.00.
5	He won't know ...	e	I'd look for something else.
6	You'll pass easily ...	f	I'll have time to go to the gym.

2 Choose words from the box to complete these sentences.

I'll	had	were	won't	finish	are

1 The meeting will finish at 5.00 if there .... no other items to discuss.
2 If I .... the chance I would love to work abroad.
3 If I see her .... ask her to call you.
4 We'll stay the night if we .... too late.
5 I'd sell it if I .... you.
6 If they aren't satisfied they .... buy from us again.

3 In each of these sentences there is a mistake. Correct it.

1 What will you do if you were me?
2 She'll be at the hotel by 10.00 if the plane will land on time.
3 If I could be from another country I'll like to be Italian.
4 What happen if you miss the train?
5 Come and visit us when you have time next week.
6 I'll take my laptop in case I will need to check the figures.

5 COUNTABLE AND UNCOUNTABLE NOUNS

Countable nouns

1 Most nouns in English are countable and have a singular and a plural form.
job ➔ *jobs* *employee* ➔ *employees*

2 To express quantity we use *many* or *a lot*. We usually use *many* in negatives and questions. To express small quantities we use *a few*.
How ***many employees*** *are there in your company?*
There are ***a lot of people*** *here.*
We only have ***a few*** *new* ***people*** *this year.*

3 We use the indefinite article with singular countable nouns (*a* / *an*).
There is ***a file*** *on my desk.*

4 In the plural we use *some* in positive sentences, or *any* in negatives and questions.
There are ***some files*** *on my desk.*
*There are****n't any vacancies.***
Are *there* ***any messages*** *for me?*

Uncountable nouns

1 Some nouns are uncountable and have no plural.
~~*informations*~~ ➔ *information* ~~*luggages*~~ ➔ *luggage*

2 They always take a singular verb.
The ***luggage is*** *in the lobby.*
There ***is*** *a lot of* ***work*** *to be done.*

3 To express quantity we use *much* or *a lot*. We usually use *much* in negatives and questions. For small quantities we use *a little*.
How ***much luggage*** *have you got?*
We've only got ***a little space.***
There is ***not much time.***

4 We cannot use an indefinite article *(a / an)* with uncountable nouns. Instead, we use *some* in positive sentences, and *any* in negatives and questions.
I've got ***some news.***
*There is****n't any petrol.***
Is *there* ***any money*** *in that account?*

Nouns that are both countable and uncountable

1 Some nouns can be countable or uncountable depending on the meaning.
Could we have two ***teas,*** *please?* (cups of tea – countable)
We need to buy some ***tea.*** (substance – uncountable)
How much ***time*** *have we got?* (length of time – uncountable)
How many ***times*** *a week do you work late?* (occasions – countable)

COMMON ERRORS

~~*How much people work here?*~~ ➔ *How many people work here?*
~~*Can I have one information, please?*~~ ➔ *Can I have some information, please?*

CHECK YOUR UNDERSTANDING

1 Are these words countable (C) or uncountable (U)?

1	machine	5	child ....
2	woman	6	stationery ....
3	music	7	progress ....
4	money	8	help ....

2 Complete these sentences with one of the words from **1** in the correct form.

1 Have you made any .... on the project?
2 How much .... did you invest?
3 I'm very busy today. Could you give me some ....?
4 Four of our .... are out of order.
5 We have five .... in our team and just two men.

3 Choose words from the box to complete these sentences.

an	some	any	few	much	many	little

1 There aren't .... vacancies at the moment. None at all.
2 How .... time do we need for this meeting?
3 I found .... interesting information on your website.
4 Have you got .... agenda?
5 A .... people are sick this week so we are very busy.
6 Are there .... flights tomorrow to Frankfurt?
7 How .... emails do you get each day?
8 We only have a .... money in our advertising budget.

Present continuous

1 We use the present continuous when we have a definite time for a future action.
*We **are having** our conference in Croatia next year.*
*She's **coming** here on the 5th.*

Will

1 We use *will / won't* to make a general prediction about the future.
*In 2020 we **will use** different forms of transport.*
*This new product **won't be** as good as the old one.*

2 We use *will* to make a decision at the moment of speaking.
A *We'd like to offer you the job.*
B ***I'll take** it.*
A *Could someone answer the door?*
B ***I'll get** it.*

3 We use *will* in conditional sentences.
*If you win the contract, **I'll buy** you a bottle of champagne.*

4 Form: *will / won't* + infinitive.

Going to

1 We use *going to* to talk about our intentions.
*Sales are down. What **are we going to do**?*
*We'**re going to invite** all our customers to a party.*

2 We use *going to* to predict something from a present situation.
*There is a lot on the agenda. It's **going to be** a long meeting.*

3 Form: present tense of *be* + *going to* + infinitive.

COMMON ERROR

~~I will to do it.~~ → *I will do it.*

CHECK YOUR UNDERSTANDING

1 Complete this conversation with the correct form of the verb in brackets.

A We have a visitor this week. The European Sales Manager!
B When (come) [1] ....?
A On Tuesday.
B What does he want to visit?
A Everything. If there are any problems I (be) [2] .... in trouble.
B (go) [3] .... to the factory?
A Yes, probably on Thursday.
B I (telephone) [4] .... the plant manager to brief him.
A Good idea.
B What (do) [5] .... here?
A He's going to visit all departments and speak to all the managers.

2 Match the sentences a–d below to these situations 1–4.

1 The telephone is ringing but your colleague is busy. ....
2 You are discussing your weekend plans with a colleague. ....
3 You are discussing your new boss with a colleague. ....
4 You are negotiating to buy some new chairs for your office. ....
a We're going to the new Italian restaurant on Saturday.
b If I buy twenty what will the price be?
c She's going to make a lot of changes.
d I'll get it.

7 MODALS

1 We use modal verbs to express ideas like ability, permission, obligation, certainty. We also use them to make requests, offers, and suggestions, or to give advice.

Talking about ability

*She **can** speak Japanese.*
*He **can't** drive.*

Asking for, giving, or refusing permission – *can* / *can't*

***Can** I leave early?*	*Of course you **can**.*
*We **can't** receive personal telephone calls in our office.*	*Nor **can** we.*

Making requests

When we ask for something politely we use *could*.

***Could** you help me?* *
***Could** I ask a question?*

Can is a little less formal.

***Can** you lend me some money?*
***Can** I use your telephone?*

Replying positively:
Yes, of course.
Certainly.
Go ahead.

Replying negatively:
I'm afraid I'm busy.
Sorry, I can't.
I'm afraid not.

Talking about obligation and necessity

1 We use *must* to give orders, or to talk about things that we think are necessary.
*You **mustn't** drink alcohol at work.*
*You **must** be punctual if you want to give a good impression.*

2 We use *have to* to talk about things that are necessary because of the situation, or another person's rules.
*We don't **have to** work in the evenings now that there are more staff.*
*Do I **have to** finish this today?*

3 There is no past or future form of *must*. We use *had to* and *will have to*.
*Last year I **had to** work really hard.*
*Next year **I'll have to** travel abroad a lot.*

4 Form: *can / could / must / shall / should / may / might / would* + infinitive.

COMMON ERROR

~~*You must to finish your work now.*~~ → *You must finish your work now.*

CHECK YOUR UNDERSTANDING

Complete these sentences with the correct modal.

1 I forgot to go to the bank. .... you lend me some money?
2 I'm sorry I .... go to lunch. I must finish this report.
3 I need to call my boss. .... I use your phone?
4 This is urgent. The report .... to go in the post tonight.
5 I'm leaving early today because last night I .... to work late.
6 If you hear the alarm you .... leave the building immediately.
7 .... I smoke? Sorry, this is a no-smoking building.
8 You .... do that. It's really dangerous.

8 PASSIVES

1 We use the passive when we do not know or it is not important to say who has done something.
*We **are paid** monthly.*
*A service charge **is included**.*

2 We often use the passive to describe processes.
*First the solution **is heated** to 150°.*
*All our products **are checked** then **packaged**.*

3 We form the passive with different tenses of the verb *be*, depending on whether the action is in the past, present, or future.

Present simple passive

*These cars **are made** in Japan.*
Form: present simple of *be* + past participle (+ *by* + noun).

Past simple passive

*Sixteen people **were recruited** last year.*
Form: *was / were* + past participle (+ *by* + noun).

Future passive

*Shoplifters **will be prosecuted**.*
Form: *will be* + past participle (+ *by* + noun).

CHECK YOUR UNDERSTANDING

1 Put these sentences in the correct order.

1 the English all world spoken is over.
2 washrooms this cleaned morning The were.
3 France Camembert made in is.
4 in brochures will be China Our printed.
5 are Porsche manufactured Stuttgart cars in.
6 emails day Millions are of sent every.

2 Make these active sentences passive.

1 We include wine and coffee in our price.
2 We import our components from Poland.
3 We make our shoes by hand.
4 My colleague painted that picture.
5 They dismissed two of my colleagues last month.
6 They will print the book in China.

9 PAST SIMPLE

1 We use the past simple to describe an action or a series of actions which happened at a particular time in the past.
*They sent the parcel on Monday but it **didn't arrive** until Friday.*

2 Here are some rules for forming the past simple in positive sentences.

Regular verbs	add *-ed*	*We start**ed** work at 7.00 yesterday.*
Regular verbs ending in *-e*	add *-d*	*She live**d** in Switzerland.*
Regular verbs ending in consonant + *-y*	change *-y* to *-i* and add *-ed*	*He tr**ied** to find a new job.*
Regular short verbs ending in vowel + consonant	double the final consonant	*I stop**ped** the car.*

3 Negatives and questions are formed in the same way for both regular and irregular verbs.

*They **didn't go**.*

*They **didn't see** the manager.*

*Where **did** they **fly** from?*

*When **did** they **arrive**?*

For a list of irregular verbs see page 121.

COMMON ERRORS

~~Where you went?~~ → *Where did you go?*

~~I have joined the company in 1998.~~ → *I joined the company in 1998.*

~~She replyed to my letter.~~ → *She replied to my letter.*

CHECK YOUR UNDERSTANDING

1 Complete this text with the correct form of the verbs in brackets.

Last week I (be) [1] .... very busy. On Monday our largest customer (visit) [2] .... our factory.
I (meet) [3] .... her at the airport at 7.00 in the morning and (take) [4] .... her to the plant. In the afternoon we (have) [5] .... a long meeting with her and in the evening she (want) [6] .... to see a show.
On Tuesday I (fly) [7] .... to Berlin for a conference. In the afternoon I (make) [8] .... a presentation and the next day I (go) [9] .... to Stuttgart to meet a supplier. On Thursday we (interview) [10] .... candidates for the new sales jobs and in the evening I (play) [11] .... squash in the company tournament. On Friday I (reply) [12] .... to my emails and (write) [13] .... a proposal for an Austrian company. In the afternoon I (attend) [14] .... the planning meeting which (finish) [15] .... at 7.30. I (buy) [16] .... a pizza on the way home and (watch) [17] .... a DVD until about 11.00. I (spend) [18] .... the weekend playing golf and relaxing. On Sunday evening I (pack) [19] .... my suitcase and (leave) [20] .... for the airport at about 8.00.

2 Complete these sentences with the past simple form of the verb in brackets.

1 (We / not / see) We ...didn't see... you at the conference.
2 What time (you / arrive) ....?
3 (They / not / reply) .... to my letter.
4 (I / leave) .... my passport at Reception.
5 Who (you / meet) .... on the trip?
6 (I / see) .... my colleague in the hotel.

Present simple

1 We use the present simple to describe facts and permanent states. These can include: job responsibilities, a company's usual activity, plane and train times.

*A bookshop **sells** books.*

*My secretary **speaks** Chinese.*

2 We can use the present simple to talk about regular actions.
*I **don't have** breakfast.*
We go to the gym every day.

3 Verbs ending in *-o* take *-es* in the third person singular.
do → does   *go → goes*
*He **goes** to work by car.*
*She **doesn't like** the hotel.*

4 With the verb *be*, and with modal verbs, we don't use *do* and *does*.
*Where's your car? I **mustn't** forget to fax the letter.*

COMMON ERRORS

~~*Where you live?*~~ → *Where do you live?*
~~*They don't be in the office.*~~ → *They aren't in the office.*
~~*I don't can speak Japanese.*~~ → *I can't speak Japanese.*

PRESENT CONTINUOUS

1 We use the present continuous to describe actions in progress at the moment of speaking. For example: our present work projects, new developments in business.

2 We also use the present continuous to talk about actions that are happening for a limited time around now.
*They **are working** in Europe until December.*
***I'm calling** you from Paris.*
*We **are working** on a new prototype at the moment.*
*She **is spending** three months here on a placement.*

3 Form: present simple of *be* + *-ing* form.

COMMON ERRORS

~~*I am often travelling.*~~ → *I often travel.*
~~*At the moment he speaks to his boss.*~~ → *At the moment he's speaking to his boss.*

CHECK YOUR UNDERSTANDING

1 Choose words from the box to complete these sentences.

don't	do	doesn't	does	finish	finishes	is	isn't	have	*has*

1 The company ......has...... three main divisions.
2 I .... my own office.
3 What time .... you usually .... work in the evening?
4 A Where .... she?
  B I don't know. She .... in her office.
5 The concert .... at about 11.15 p.m.
6 A .... the new product have a name yet?
  B No, it .... The Marketing Department is working on it now.

2 Complete the sentences with the present continuous form of the words in brackets as in the example.

1 (We / develop) *We are developing* a new range of products for South America.
2 (he / stay) .... at the Galaxie Hotel?
3 (You / not / listen) .... to me. What did I just say?
4 (I / leave) .... now. See you tomorrow morning.
5 A Why (those German engineers / visit) .... the company?
B (They / study) .... our production methods.
6 (I / not / work) .... this week – I'm on holiday.

3 In each sentence or conversation, one of the verbs in *italics* is in the wrong form. Underline the incorrect form and correct it.

1 A What *are you doing*? *do you do*
B I'm a doctor. I *work* for a research institute.
2 The painters *are re-decorating* our offices, so I *work* at home today.
3 A *Is* she always *working* long hours?
B No, not all the time. But she'*s finishing* a very important project this week.
4 The company *is* usually *spending* 2% of its budget on training, but this year it *is increasing* it to 2.6%.
5 A We'*re expanding* our activities overseas at the moment.
B Oh really? Which new countries *do* you *export* to?
6 I *don't like* going to parties usually, but I really *enjoy* this one.

11 PRESENT PERFECT

1 We use the present perfect to talk about an action or series of actions in the past, especially if there is a connection with the present.
The plane ***has landed****.* (it is on the ground now)

2 We can use the present perfect to describe a situation or action which began in the past, but which continues into the present.
I've worked *for my present company since 2002.*

3 We often use the present perfect with *already*, *yet*, *ever*, *never*, and *just*.
We use *ever* / *never* to talk about something that has (not) happened during our life.
Have you ***ever*** *used a private jet for business travel?*
I have ***never*** *worked so hard.*
We use *just* in positive present perfect sentences to mean a short time before now.
I've ***just*** *seen my old boss.*
We use *already* to talk about something that happened before we expected.
He's ***already*** *arrived.*
We use *yet* in questions and negative sentences to ask if something expected has happened, or to say that it hasn't.
Haven't you finished ***yet****?*
She hasn't called me ***yet****.*

4 We often use *for* and *since* to talk about unfinished actions.

For + period of time.

She has worked here ***for*** *three years.* (she still works here)

Since + a particular point in time.

He has been my boss ***since*** *the start of the year.* (he is still my boss)

5 To describe a finished action we use the past simple.

I worked in Australia in the 1990s. (I do not work there now)

She was my boss from 1987 to 1995. (she is not my boss now)

In a positive sentence we put *already*, *never*, and *just* between *have* and the past participle.

You have ***never*** *told me that.*

He / She has ***just*** *left.*

I have ***already*** *had lunch.*

6 Form: present tense of *have* + past participle.

COMMON ERRORS

~~She has written the report yesterday.~~ → *She wrote the report yesterday.*

~~He works here since three years.~~ → *He has worked here for three years.*

CHECK YOUR UNDERSTANDING

1 Complete these sentences with the correct form of the verb in brackets.

1 There are four candidates. So far we (interview) ...have interviewed... two of them.
2 Our Marketing Director is visiting clients this week. She (see) .... five of them.
3 (meet) .... you .... my colleague?
4 I started playing golf recently. I (play) ....about ten times.
5 We are mailing four thousand brochures. We (already / send) .... two thousand.
6 He is applying for a new job. He (write) .... about fifty letters.

2 Complete these questions and answers.

1 You / see Ann? ...Have you seen Ann?...
Yes, I saw her half an hour ago in the canteen.
2 He / write the report? ....?
Yes, he wrote it yesterday.
3 They / leave? ....?
Yes, they left ten minutes ago.
4 You / ever / travel first class? ....?
Yes, I have.
5 The meeting / finish? ....?
Yes, it has just finished.

3 Read this postcard from a sales representative to her colleagues from a business trip abroad. Complete it with the correct form of the verbs in brackets.

Dear All,
I (arrive) 1 .... here a week ago and I am working really hard. I (visit) 2 .... several big customers and I (already / find) 3 .... a new one. I (try) 4 .... lots of the local cooking and I must say I (never eat) 5 .... so well. I (just finish) 6 .... dinner and am now going out to see a film. I (meet) 7 .... a couple of other people yesterday so I am not completely alone. See you all next week.
Regards,
Felicity.

12 PREPOSITIONS OF PLACE AND DIRECTION

1

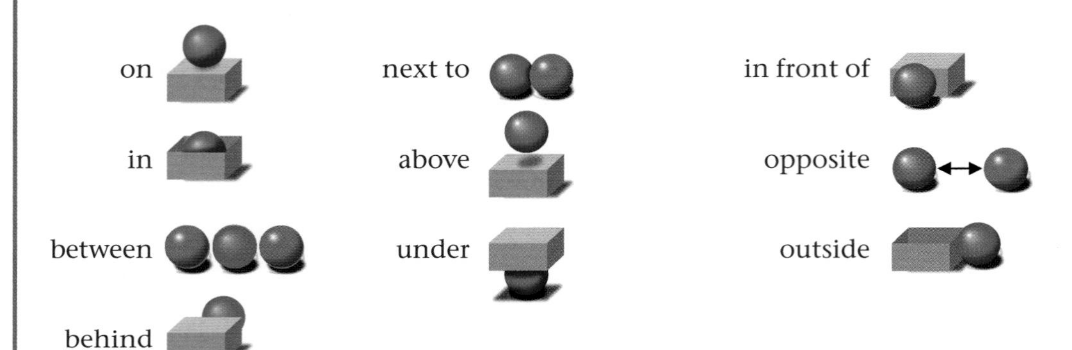

CHECK YOUR UNDERSTANDING

Complete these sentences with one of the prepositions.

1 My office is .... the main building .... the fourth floor.
2 The stationery cupboard is .... the door and the wall.
3 The keyboard is usually .... the screen.
4 The mouse is usually .... the keyboard.
5 .... is the opposite of *over*.

13 PREPOSITIONS OF TIME

1 We generally use the following prepositions before the following things.

in times of the day – *in the morning, in the afternoon, in the evening*
seasons – *the spring, the summer, the autumn, the winter*
months – *January, February, March*

on days of the week – *Monday, Tuesday* (NB no preposition in US)
the weekend (US)

at times – *five o'clock, half past six, midnight*
the weekend (UK)

from ➔ *She works from 9 to 5* ➔ **to**

since a point in time *I've been here* ***since eight o'clock.***

for a period of time *They waited* ***for four hours*** *for their plane.*

until a point in time *We worked* ***until nine*** *to get ready for the meeting.*

CHECK YOUR UNDERSTANDING

Complete this text with the correct preposition.

Romain Candella works for a fireworks company. He has worked there [1] .... 1997. Before that he worked as a waiter [2] .... five years. As a waiter he worked [3] .... eleven in the morning [4] .... nine or ten [5] .... night. These days he works a normal day and never works [6] ....the weekend. His busiest time is [7] .... the autumn. [8] ....November 5th his sales reach a peak. After that it is quiet [9] .... Christmas. He usually goes on holiday [10] .... the spring.

14 PRONOUNS

1

SUBJECT PRONOUNS	OBJECT PRONOUNS	POSSESSIVE PRONOUNS	POSSESSIVE ADJECTIVES
I	me	mine	my
you	you	yours	your
he	him	his	his
she	her	hers	her
it	it	its	its
we	us	ours	our
they	them	theirs	their

CHECK YOUR UNDERSTANDING

Complete these sentences using one of the words in the table above.

1 Could I borrow .... telephone? .... has no battery.
2 My wife works very long hours. .... is a doctor. .... colleagues work much less.
3 He lost .... job last year. I feel very sorry for ....
4 Would you like some oysters? No thanks. I don't like ....
5 Whose laptop is this? It's .... Where is ....?

15 QUESTIONS

1 To form questions in the present simple and past simple we use the auxiliary *do / does / did*.

***Do** you work here?*

***Does** she speak Japanese?*

*What time **did** you leave?*

2 We do not use an auxiliary with the verb *be*, or with modal verbs.

Is she Dutch?

Where were you yesterday?

3 We usually put a preposition at the end of a question.

*Which company do you work **for**?*

*Who did you have lunch **with**?*

*Where are you **from**?*

4 For other tenses or modals we invert the subject and the auxiliary.

*What **will you** do?*

*Where **can I** find a new supplier?*

*How long **have you** worked here?*

5 We use question tags to check or confirm information. When the auxiliary is positive in the sentence, it is negative in the tag.
They live in Italy, ***don't they?***
They came yesterday, ***didn't they?***
She can go the meeting, ***can't she?***
You were there last year, ***weren't you?***
She has left, ***hasn't she?***

6 In a negative sentence the question tag is usually positive.
He can't sign company cheques, ***can he?***
They haven't left, ***have they?***

CHECK YOUR UNDERSTANDING

1 Make questions for the words in **bold**.

1 They live in **Barcelona**. — *Where do they live?*
2 I work for **Qantas**. — Which company ....?
3 She goes to work **by car**. — How ....?
4 He earns **$50,000** a year. — How much ....?
5 We start work at **8.30**. — What time ....?
6 I have lunch **in the company canteen**. — Where ....?

2 Complete the gaps in these questions.

1 Where .... you meet? At a conference in Miami in 1999.
2 Where .... you yesterday? At a meeting in Manchester.
3 When .... the meeting start? At 2 o'clock.
4 .... she French? No, she isn't. She's Swiss.
5 Why .... she fax you? Because the computers are down.
6 How many people .... there? There were six of us.

3 Match the questions 1–6 with the answers a–f.

1	Who did you have dinner with?	a	They're discussing prices.
2	What are you working on?	b	Wood.
3	What is it for?	c	It's the news.
4	What is it made of?	d	Next year's budget.
5	What are you listening to?	e	It's for cleaning your keyboard.
6	What are they talking about?	f	A Spanish customer.

4 Make question tags for these sentences.

1 She works hard, *doesn't she?*
2 They live in Melbourne, ...?
3 He went by train, ...?
4 She's got a new job, ...?
5 He didn't telephone, ...?
6 You're new, ...?

16 IRREGULAR VERB LIST

Infinitive	Past simple	Past participle	Infinitive	Past simple	Past participle
be	was / were	been	let	let	let
become	became	become	lose	lost	lost
begin	began	begun	make	made	made
break	broke	broken	mean	meant	meant
bring	brought	brought	meet	met	met
build	built	built	pay	paid	paid
buy	bought	bought	put	put	put
catch	caught	caught	read	read	read
choose	chose	chosen	ring	rang	rung
come	came	come	rise	rose	risen
cost	cost	cost	run	ran	run
cut	cut	cut	say	said	said
deal	dealt	dealt	see	saw	seen
do	did	done	sell	sold	sold
draw	drew	drawn	send	sent	sent
drink	drank	drunk	set	set	set
drive	drove	driven	show	showed	shown
eat	ate	eaten	shut	shut	shut
fall	fell	fallen	sing	sang	sung
feel	felt	felt	sleep	slept	slept
find	found	found	speak	spoke	spoken
fly	flew	flown	spend	spent	spent
forget	forgot	forgotten	stand	stood	stood
get	got	got	steal	stole	stolen
give	gave	given	stick	stuck	stuck
go	went	been / gone	strike	struck	struck
grow	grew	grown	swim	swam	swum
have	had	had	take	took	taken
hear	heard	heard	teach	taught	taught
hold	held	held	tell	told	told
keep	kept	kept	think	thought	thought
know	knew	known	throw	threw	thrown
lead	led	led	wake	woke	woken
learn	learned / learnt	learned / learnt	wear	wore	worn
leave	left	left	win	won	won
lend	lent	lent	write	wrote	written

17 MEETINGS, OPINIONS, AND SUGGESTIONS

USEFUL LANGUAGE AND EXPRESSIONS

Opening a meeting
Thanks for coming.
Has everyone got an agenda?
Right. Shall we start?

Asking for opinions
What do you think?
Would you like to comment / say something?
Does anyone want to add anything?
Don't you think ...?
Don't you agree?

Giving opinions
I think ...
In my opinion ...
To my mind ...
From my point of view ...
I feel (very strongly) ...
On the one hand ... on the other ...

Agreeing / disagreeing
I agree.
That's a good point.
I disagree.
I'm not sure about that.
I don't fully agree with you.
I take your point but ...

Making suggestions
Why don't we ...?
What about + -ing?
Let's ...
We could ...

Commenting
Good idea!
Great!
No way!

Checking understanding
I didn't catch that.
I'm not with you.

Ending
I think that's enough for today.
Any other business?
Thanks for coming / your attention.

18 TELEPHONE LANGUAGE

Making calls
Introducing yourself
This is Thomas Lund.
(It's) Thomas Lund here.

Receiving calls
Answering the phone
Rosemary Patricot. How can I help?
Rosemary Patricot speaking.

Asking for someone
Can I speak to Lucy Adams, please?
Is Lucy Adams there?
Is that Lucy?

Transferring
Just a moment. I'll put you through.
I'll try another number.

Leaving a message
Can I leave a message?
Could you tell her Thomas phoned?
I'll call back tomorrow.

Taking a message
Can I take a message?
How do you spell that?
Has she got your number?

Apologizing
I'm afraid she's out.
Sorry. She's not at her desk.

Ending a call

Thanks for your help.
Speak to you soon.
Bye for now.

Thanks for calling.
Nice talking to you.
Bye bye.

19 MAKING APPOINTMENTS

Asking when a person is free

When are you available?
Which day is good for you?

Responding

Any morning.
I'm free on Tuesday.

Suggesting a date

Are you free on the fourteenth?
Does Friday suit you?

Rejecting

Sorry, I'm busy that day.
I'm afraid I'm away.

Suggesting a time

Is three o'clock OK for you?
Shall we say half past four?

Accepting

That's fine.
All right.

Confirming

So that's 4.30 on Monday the tenth.

Acknowledging

OK. I look forward to it.

Changing

I've got a problem with our appointment. Can we postpone it / bring it forward / cancel it?

20 SOCIAL EXPRESSIONS

Meeting people for the first time

Hello.
How are you?
Where are you from?

Meeting colleagues

Hi.
How are you doing?
How's the family?
How are things?

Asking for help

Could you give me a hand?
Can you help me?
I was wondering if you could do something for me.

Offering

Can I do anything?
How can I help?
Shall I do that?

Inviting

Are you doing anything now / later / this evening?
Would you like to have dinner with us?
Are you free later?
Have you got any plans?

Asking for directions

Excuse me? Could you tell me how to get to ...?
Do you know where ... street is?
Is there a garage near here?
Where can I find ...?

Complaining

This is too ... .
This is not ... enough.
Sorry, but there seems to be a mistake.

Saying goodbye

It was great to see you again.
Thanks for the invitation.
Thanks for coming.
See you soon.
Bye for now.

Apologizing

I do apologize.
I am so / really sorry.

21 WRITING BUSINESS CORRESPONDENCE

1 We use different expressions when we write formal letters (to institutions or companies), and informal letters (to friends or emails to colleagues).

	Formal letter	**Email / Informal letter**
Opening	*Dear Sir / Madam* *Dear Sirs*	*Dear Nadia / Hi Nadia*
Reference	*With reference to ...*	(Email: appears in subject box) *I am writing to ...*
Thanks	*Thank you for ...*	*Thanks for ...*
Enclosed	*Please find enclosed ...*	*Attached is / are ...* *Please find attached ...*
Asking for help	*I would be grateful if you could ...*	*Could / Can you ...?*
Offering help	*I would be pleased to ...*	*I'll / I'd be pleased to ...* *I'd be glad to ...*
Closing remark	*I look forward to hearing from you.*	*Looking forward to hearing from you.* *Hope to hear from you soon.*
Finishing	*Yours faithfully,* *Yours sincerely,*	*Kindest /Best regards,* *Yours,*

22 NUMBERS

1 **Cardinal numbers**

1–10	one, two, three, four, five, six, seven, eight, nine, ten
11–20	eleven, twelve, thirteen, fourteen, fifteen, sixteen, seventeen, eighteen, nineteen, twenty
21–29	twenty-one, twenty-two, twenty-three ... twenty-nine
30–90	thirty, forty, fifty, sixty, seventy, eighty, ninety
100	a hundred, or one hundred
137	a hundred (and) thirty-seven
7,926	seven thousand nine hundred and twenty-six
12,456	twelve thousand four hundred and fifty-six
348,931	three hundred and forty-eight thousand, nine hundred and thirty-one

2,345,678	two million, three hundred and forty-five thousand six hundred and seventy-eight
1,000,000,000	one billion

2 **Ordinal numbers**

1	1st (first)
2	2nd (second)
3	3rd (third)
4–9	4th, 5th ... 9th (fourth, fifth ... ninth)
10–19	10th (tenth), 11th (eleventh), 12th (twelfth) ... 19th (nineteenth)
20–100	20th (twentieth), 30th (thirtieth) ... 90th (ninetieth), 100th (hundredth)

3 **Fractions**

$\frac{1}{2}$	a half
$\frac{1}{3}$	a third
$\frac{1}{4}$	a quarter
$\frac{1}{5} - \frac{1}{100}$	a fifth ... a hundredth

4 **Other numbers**

59%	Fifty-nine per cent
1.056	One point zero / nought / oh, five, six
6.8	Six point eight
77°	Seventy-seven degrees
$\frac{7}{10}$	Seven-tenths

5 **Dates**

What is the date? What is the year? When were you born? When did it happen?

2003	Two thousand and three
1998	Nineteen ninety-eight
1666	Sixteen sixty-six
11/06/02	*The eleventh of June, two thousand and two.* *June (the) eleventh, two thousand and two.*

Note: in the US this date is written month / day / year, i.e. 06/11/02.

6 **Age**

How old is she?	*She's thirty-five (years old).*
How old is this building?	*It's two hundred years old.*

7 **Dimensions**

Distance	*How far is it from A to B? Oxford is fifty miles from London.*
Weight	*How much does he weigh? He weighs seventy-five kilos.*
Height	*How tall is she? She's 1.60m. She's one metre-sixty.*
Dimensions	*How big is your office? My office is six metres by four.*
Time	*It's six forty-five. (6.45)*

8 Time

What time is it?
What's the time?
What time do you have? (US)
What time do you make it? (UK)

On the hour.	*It's one, two, three o'clock.*
From 1 minute to 30 minutes *after* the hour.	*It's ten, quarter, twenty-five, half,* ***past*** *four. (UK)* *It's ten, quarter, twenty-five, half* ***after*** *four. (US)*
From 29 minutes to 1 minute *before* the hour.	*It's ten, quarter, twenty-five* ***to*** *four. (UK)* *It's a quarter, half* ***of*** *four. (US)*
We can also say:	*It's ten thirty-three. It's six forty-five.*

We usually use the 24-hour clock when we are talking about timetables.

My plane goes at 19.30.	*My plane goes at nineteen thirty.*
The conference ends at 18.30.	*The conference ends at eighteen thirty.*

9 Telephone numbers and postcodes

0033153594443	*That's oh, oh, three, three, one, five, three, five, nine, double four, four, three.*
44000	*That's four, four, oh, oh, oh.*
OX14 6QT	*Oh, ex, one, four, six, queue, tea.*

10 Prices

How much is that?
What does it cost?
How much do I owe you?

€6.50	*Six euros fifty.*
£78.35	*Seventy-eight pounds thirty-five (pence).*

CHECK YOUR UNDERSTANDING

Write the answers to these questions in words.

1. How old are you? *Thirty-five.*
2. When were you born?
3. How many people work for your company?
4. What is the average salary in your country?
5. How tall are you?
6. What's your postcode?
7. What's your phone number?
8. What time is it?
9. What is the exchange rate between the dollar and the euro?
10. How much is a coffee in a café in your town?

Tapescript

UNIT 1

(((1.1)))

Interviewer So, who do you work for?
Employee I work for Candy-Hoover.
Interviewer Where do you work?
Employee I work at the head office in Brugherio, near Milan.
Interviewer What sort of company is it? Public, private?
Employee It's a family business. But quite a large one. We have about 6,700 employees.
Interviewer What does the company do?
Employee You don't know? Candy-Hoover is one of Italy's most famous companies. We manufacture white goods. Products like vacuum cleaners, dishwashers, and so on. We have a range of 1,400 different products.
Interviewer Do you have any famous brands?
Employee Yes. You probably know Iberna or Rosières, for example.
Interviewer Is the electrical domestic appliances market difficult?
Employee Oh, yes. We have many competitors in Europe and the Far East like Whirlpool, Electrolux, and Moulinex.
Interviewer And what is the turnover?
Employee Last year we had sales of about $470 million.
Interviewer How much of that turnover was in Europe?
Employee A lot. 80%.

(((1.2)))

Interviewer So, Felipe. What's your job?
Felipe I'm an accountant. I work in the Finance Department.
Interviewer And what are you working on at the moment?
Felipe I'm working on the budget for next year.
Interviewer Your English is very good.
Felipe Thanks! I have lessons every week because the subsidiaries report to me in English.
Interviewer And what about you Maria? Where do you work?
Maria I work in the Purchasing Department.
Interviewer What do you do?
Maria I'm a buyer.
Interviewer And what are you working on today?
Maria Well, I'm trying to find a supplier for some fabric we need for a new design.
Interviewer And do you study English?
Maria Yes. I'm preparing for an exam.
Interviewer ... and what about you Henri?
Henri I'm a manager in the Personnel Department. I'm busy recruiting new people for our Logistics Department.
Interviewer And do you study English too?
Henri Yes, but I'm too busy to study here so I go to England for two weeks every year. I need to because I attend a lot of meetings in English.
Interviewer Thank you all very much.

(((1.3)))

Tom Hello. What's your name?
Silvia Silvia, Silvia Riva.
Tom Nice to meet you. I'm Tom Wilkes. So, what do you do, Silvia?
Silvia I'm a doctor.
Tom Oh, and who do you work for?
Silvia I work for a Swiss pharmaceutical company.
Tom Right. What department do you work in?
Silvia I'm in the Research Department.
Tom And what are you working on at the moment?
Silvia We're working on a new anti-stress drug.
Tom And what are you doing here at the conference?
Silvia I'm giving two papers and attending some workshops.
Tom Are you enjoying your stay?
Silvia Yes, I am, thank you.
Tom Nice meeting you.
Silvia Yes, you too.

(((1.4)))

a Of course you can. Black with two sugars?
b Yes, it's half past five.
c Of course. What would you like to know?
d Yes of course. Can I take your number, please?
e I said my name is Jones. J-O-N-E-S.
f Sorry. I've got a meeting in five minutes.
g I'm afraid he's having lunch. Could you call back later?
h Certainly madam. Straight down this corridor, on the left.

(((1.5)))

Receptionist Life Health Clubs. How can I help?
George Hi. This is George Lawrence. I'm calling from Washington. Could I speak to the Marketing Director, please?
Receptionist I'm afraid he's in a meeting all day. Can I take a message, Mr Lawrence?
George How about the Sales Director?
Receptionist Hold the line, please ... I'm sorry Mr Lawrence, but his line is busy. Can I help?
George Well, I'm trying to arrange a visit to your company for an article I'm writing on health clubs around the world.
Receptionist In that case I'll put you through to our Public Relations Department. One second, please.
Marie-Claire Public Relations. Marie-Claire speaking. How can I help?

(((1.6)))

A I think our new product range is really excellent.
B Me too, but how are we telling people about it?
A Well, first of all, we are sending an email to everyone on the database.
B I think people get too many emails these days. Aren't we updating the website too?

A It is up to date. Anyway, I don't think many of our customers visit it.
B Maybe you're right. So are we doing anything else?
A Yes, we're organizing an event to present our new range of products.
B OK. Who are we inviting? Large customers, small customers?
A Everybody, but first we must see if they are interested. We're sending out an invitation to an open day in July. Can you design a nice invitation?
B Sure. Let's meet up again tomorrow.

UNIT 2

2.1

A So, how did you have the idea of green ketchup?
B The original idea came from children who wanted more fun when eating. Our research team did some research to see if it was possible to produce green sauce.
A What happened after that?
B We trialed it. The trials lasted several months. We used the results of this research to improve the product as much as we could. When we were happy with the taste and the colour, we were ready to brand it.
A You didn't call it 'ketchup'?
B No. We wanted a special name for kids and we decided on the brand name 'EZ Squirt'.
A What about the bottle design?
B In tests we saw that kids needed a special bottle. We designed about ten different bottles and then we tested them to find the right size and shape. As you can see, the EZ Squirt bottle is a very new design.
A What was the next stage?
B We costed the product.
A It's more expensive than regular ketchup, isn't it?
B Yes, but it has extra vitamins and comes in smaller bottles.
A And the final stages?
B We talked to the press and started to advertise it. The launch was in Pittsburgh in October 2000, and by the start of 2001 it was on sale throughout the country.

2.2

A Could you tell us a little more about the company's history?
B Sure. The next big landmark was 1988.
A What happened?
B We produced our 2 millionth Xerox copier!
A 2 millionth? That's incredible.
B In 1994 we decided to change things just a little. We introduced our new logo – the red X. Red then became our corporate colour replacing blue.
A I see. What about your involvement in Ireland?
B Yes, in 1998 we announced plans to open a manufacturing site in Dundalk and a call centre in Dublin. Then, of course, we were a major sponsor at the Olympic Games in Sydney. We burned all the results on CD-ROMs to make electronic results books.
A Really? So what happened next?
B Well, in 2002 a woman became Chairman of Xerox for the first time!
A Wow! That was a big change I imagine?
B It certainly was!

2.3

1

Tanja Excuse me? Is this seat free?
Victoria Yes, sure. Is this your first day?
Tanja Yes, it is.
Victoria Where are you working?
Tanja In R&D.
Victoria Really? Who's your boss?
Tanja I'm working with Katya Ramirez.
Victoria Oh, I know her. She's nice. I'm Victoria by the way.
Tanja Nice to meet you. I'm Tanja. Tanja Johannsen.
Victoria Nice to meet you too.

2

Michael Good evening.
Graham Hello.
Michael My name's Graf. Michael Graf.
Graham Pleased to meet you. I'm Graham Turner.
Michael Where do you work?
Graham I'm from the Amsterdam office. What about you?
Michael Munich. Is this your first visit to Italy?
Graham No, I came to this conference last year. Are you new?
Michael Yes. I started in February.
Graham Do you know many people here?
Michael Not really.
Graham In that case, let me introduce you to some people. Come on!

3

Tony Excuse me?
Hanni Yes?
Tony Your face is familiar. Have we met?
Hanni Yes, I think we have.
Tony Ah, when you came in I thought I recognized you. Who do you work for, again?
Hanni I work for UBS in Zurich. What about you?
Tony Me too. Which department are you in?
Hanni I'm an auditor. I work in Internal Audit.
Tony That's where we met. I work in the Training Department and you did an audit two years ago.
Hanni Ah, yes. Now I remember.

2.4

1

A Did you see the match last night?
B Which one?
A The men's semi-final. It was a fabulous game. It lasted about three hours.
B Really? I didn't see it. I was out. I don't really like tennis.

2

C Do you like reading?
D Yes I do.
C What are you reading at the moment?
D A biography. It's about Bill Clinton.
C What's it like?
D Mmm. Not bad. It's a bit long. What about you?
C I'm reading a thriller. It's set in South Africa in the fifties.
D Who's it by?
C A woman called Ella Goldsmith.

3
E Is your fish nice?
F It's fine. What about your omelette?
E Very nice. I love the herbs they put in.
F So are you a vegetarian?
E Not really. I sometimes eat meat but not often.
F Do you cook at home?
E Yes. I love it.
F What sort of things?
E Italian mainly. You know – pasta, risotto, and so on. What about you?
F I'm useless in the kitchen.

4
G Did you have a holiday last year?
H Yes we did.
G Oh, where did you go?
H We went to Greece.
G Really? Where exactly?
H One of the islands – Paxos.
G Oh? Where's that?
H Quite near Corfu. What about you?
G Mauritius!
H Wow! Wasn't it expensive to go there?
G It wasn't cheap but we wanted to try somewhere different.

2.5

1
A I'm a sales rep.
B Are you? Who do you work for?
A I'm with Buitoni. What about you?
B I work for Nestlé. I'm a research scientist.
A That's interesting. What kind of research do you do?

2
C My company's Spanish.
D Is it really? Where's it based, then?
C In Madrid.
D I see. But you don't work in Madrid.
C No, I work in our office in the south of France.

3
E I have six children.
F Do you? Gosh! How old are they?
E The eldest is twelve and the youngest is two.
F My goodness, that's a lot of work. Do you have three boys and three girls, then?
E No, they're all boys. We're still trying for a girl!

4
G I love pasta.
H Me too. What's your favourite dish, then?
G Mmm, lasagne I think.
H Yes, I love that too. Do you cook a lot, then?
G No, only when I have the time. At weekends, for example.

5
I I worked in the USA for three years.
J Did you? That's interesting. Where were you?
I In New York. I worked for a bank.
J So why did you leave?
I I didn't like the lifestyle there.

6
K I don't like football.
L Me neither. What sports are you interested in, then?
K Mainly racquet sports, like tennis or badminton.
L Right. Do you play yourself?
K Well, I still play tennis a little. But less and less these days.

2.6

A What do you think about my new sunglasses?
B Very nice. Expensive were they?
A Yes, they're Oakley's. They cost over a hundred pounds.
B I paid about ten pounds for mine. From the supermarket. They're very good.
A Yes but they're not a brand are they?
B Do you always buy branded products like Heinz tomato ketchup or Wrigley's chewing gum?
A Yes, I do. I think they are better quality. And, the companies that make them have good reputations.
B But are they really better?
A Of course they are. Like Oxford dictionaries or Perrier sparkling water.
B Do you fancy a coffee?
A Yes, that would be nice. Let's go to Starbucks!
B Let's just go to that little place in town. The coffee is better and half the price.
A No, I prefer Starbucks.
B OK.

UNIT 3

3.1

a **A** We want to go to Seville on Saturday. Is there a flight that leaves at about 7 a.m.?
B Yes, there's one that leaves at 7.30. But are there any seats still free? Let me check.
b **C** How much luggage have you got? You can only take one bag on the flight.
D Well, I haven't got much to check in – I've only got this small bag and my laptop. Have you got any window seats?
c **E** I need to buy some presents. How much time do I have before we board?
F We don't have any news at the moment. All we know is that there's a delay on the incoming flight. I'm sure you'll have some time to go shopping.
d **G** How many nights would you like to stay?
H Two, please. Are there any rooms on the top floor with a view of the city? I'd like to take some photos.
e **I** Do you have any information about hotels in the city centre?
J No, but I can do some research for you. How much are you prepared to pay per night?
f **K** I need to change some money. Are there any banks near here?
L Well, there aren't any banks within walking distance, but there's a bureau de change in this hotel.

3.2

1
Ladies and gentlemen, we are now beginning our descent. Please return to your seats and fasten your seatbelts. Please switch off all electronic equipment to avoid interference with the plane's navigation systems.

2

A So, that's a single for two nights, sir?
B Yes, that's right.
A You're in room 416. Do you need help with your baggage?
B No, thanks. I can manage.
A OK, so, this is your key card ...

3

We would like to inform passengers that the 11.30 service to Indianapolis will now be departing at twelve noon from track 31. AMTRAK would like to apologize for this delay.

4

A OK madam, here's your driver's license, and here's the rental agreement.
B Thanks very much.
A You'll find it on the third floor in lot number 354.
B Great, thank you. Does it have a full tank?
A Yes, it does, madam.

5

This is the final call for passengers travelling to Brussels on flight DL167. This flight is now boarding at Gate 36. Would all remaining passengers for flight DL167 to Brussels, please proceed immediately to Gate 36.

3.3

1

A Please take a seat.
B Thanks.
A Would you like something to drink?
B No thanks, I'm fine.

2

A Thank you for coming today.
B It's a pleasure.
A Would you like me to help you with that?
B No thank you. That's OK.

3

B So this is your main factory?
A Yes, that's right. Would you like to have a look round?
B Yes, that would be nice.

4

A It's very hot in here.
B Yes, it is.
A Shall I open the window?
B Yes please, if you could.

3.4

1

A Welcome to Freebird.
B Thanks very much. It's nice to be here.

2

A Did you have a good trip?
B Yes, thanks. It was fine.

3

A And did you find your way here all right?
B No problem. Your secretary sent me a very good map.

4

A That's good. Where are you staying?
B At the Continental Hotel.

5

A So how long are you here for?
B Just three days.

6

A Would you like something to drink before we start?
B Yes, please. A coffee would be nice.

7

A OK, I'll fix that for you. Now, did you get the programme I sent you?
B Yes, I did thanks.
A Good, so perhaps we can get started.

3.5

A Welcome to Freebird.
B Thanks very much. It's nice to be here.
A Is this your first time in Lisbon?
B Yes, it is.
A Did you have a good trip?
B Yes, thanks. It was fine.
A What time did you arrive last night?
B Oh, I was at my hotel at about 8.00.
A That's good. Not too late, then. And did you find your way here all right?
B No problem. Your secretary sent me a very good map.
A That's good. How did you get here – by car?
B Yes, I rented a car at the airport.
A Where are you staying?
B At the Continental Hotel.
A And is it comfortable enough for you?
B Yes, thanks. It's very comfortable.
A I'm pleased to hear that. So how long are you here for?
B Just three days.
A And will you have time to look around Lisbon while you're here?
B Yes, I hope so.
A Well, I'm sure we can arrange something. Would you like something to drink before we start?
B Yes, please. A coffee would be nice.
A How do you like it?
B Black please, no sugar.
A OK, I'll fix that for you. Now, did you get the programme I sent you?
B Yes, I did, thanks.
A And would you like to make any changes?
B No, everything seems fine.
A Oh, good, so perhaps we can get started.

3.6

Interviewer Can you tell us something about doing business in Brazil? Is it important to arrive on time for meetings or appointments?
Interviewee Well, here, there's a difference between São Paulo and Rio de Janeiro. In São Paulo it's very important to arrive in good time. But in Rio it's normal to be up to fifteen minutes late.
Interviewer Ah, so what happens when a businessman from Rio has a meeting with one from São Paulo?
Interviewee That's a very good question! I think it probably depends where the meeting is. You also need to know that in Brazil, people often change appointments or meetings at the last

minute, or cancel them completely. So you must be ready to arrange new meetings while you're there.

Interviewer And what about the meeting or appointment itself? Can you start talking business immediately?

Interviewee No, it's very important to start with some small talk – your family, their family, the city you're in, football of course, anything that's not business. If you don't do that, your host will perhaps think that you're not interested in doing business with him.

Interviewer How easy is it to conclude a deal with a Brazilian – to sign a contract, I mean?

Interviewee The important thing here is to be patient – not to go too quickly. A Brazilian wants to know you well before doing business with you. So it's not easy to sign a contract on the first visit. You will probably have to come back to Brazil another time.

Interviewer In Europe, an important part of business culture is the business lunch, of course. Is that part of Brazilian culture too?

Interviewee Yes, very much. But remember that for a Brazilian, the idea of going to a restaurant is not to do business, but to get to know you better. But he will be very happy if you invite him for lunch, and very happy also if you ask him to choose the restaurant.

UNIT 4

4.1

A I work in Chicago and the system in my company is my employer pays 10% of my salary into the company pension scheme. How about you?

B I work for a Swedish company and we have a different system. The employer puts in exactly the same amount as we pay. For example, this year I am contributing 4% so the company pays in another 4%.

A Sounds a good system. Is it the same everywhere in Scandinavia?

B Sorry, I don't know about the other countries.

A OK. What about the working hours?

B We have to work between 10.00 and 4.00 every day. We must then do another fifteen hours in the rest of the week. What about in America?

A I work in production so I have to be there at 7.30 in the morning. I have forty-five minutes off for lunch and leave at half past four every day.

B Oh! That's a long day. What about maternity leave? How does your company deal with that?

A I think it's about eight weeks off. Then the job is kept open for about six months. Is that the same with your company?

B No. I had six months off on full pay for my first child and a year for my second! My husband had three weeks off each time as well! We have very good maternity leave in Sweden.

A That's amazing! We only get two weeks' paid holiday per year! Still, they gave me a cell phone. That way they can call me if there is a problem!

B I've got a mobile as well. I can only use it for professional calls. Or I should only use it for professional calls.

A Oh! I can use mine whenever I like and the company pays. You didn't tell me how much holiday you get, by the way.

B Six weeks a year. Plus one day per month to make up for all the extra time I do.

A Very nice! I could do with that!

4.2

Anna So it looks like we have three good applicants on the shortlist. One is local and two live abroad. Any suggestions for the next step? Marianne?

Marianne What about interviewing them by phone?

George No, I think I'd prefer to meet them in the flesh.

Marianne In that case, I think we should invite them here on different days.

George I'm not sure. Why don't we invite them here on the same day?

Anna That's a good idea but I think we probably need two days. We could have dinner together to see how they get on with people and then interview them the next day.

George How about asking them to make a short presentation about our marketing strategy?

Marianne Nice one.

Anna We could also ask them to work together on a small project to see how they work in a team.

Marianne OK. Why don't I call them today and see if we can find two free days in the next two weeks?

Anna Fine. Why don't you do that now? While you're doing that, we'll think about a project they can work on. Let's get some coffee and talk about it. Any ideas, George?

4.3

Marianne Hello, is that Mr Lawson?

Charles Speaking.

Marianne This is Marianne from Clips UK. How are you?

Charles Very well thank you.

Marianne I'm calling to tell you that you have been shortlisted for the job ...

Charles Have I? Fantastic!

Marianne Yes, congratulations! I'm now trying to arrange the second interviews here in the UK.

Charles Hang on. I'll get my diary. Right.

Marianne So, when are you free?

Charles Which week are you talking about?

Marianne Either next week, week 23, or the week after – week 24.

Charles Next week is difficult so I'd prefer the week after.

Marianne Right. That's the week beginning Monday the fourteenth. How about Tuesday the fifteenth?

Charles I'm free that day but the following day I'm in Madrid.

Marianne Are you available on the seventeenth and eighteenth?

Charles I'm afraid I'm busy on the morning of the seventeenth.

Marianne OK. So shall we say the afternoon of the seventeenth and then all day on the eighteenth?

Charles That would be fine. What time is good for you?

Marianne Late afternoon. Is four thirty OK?

Charles Four thirty'll be fine. I can leave here about eleven.
Marianne Fine. Now, I need to talk to the others before I can confirm so I'll call you back later. Is that OK?
Charles That's fine with me. I'll speak to you later.
Marianne OK. Bye.

4.4

A Hello, you're listening to Career Talk with me, Rich Green. So, next caller, good evening. How can I help?
B Evening. My problem is a bit different. I have a good job but it's not really satisfying.
A In what way?
B Well, you see, I love sailing. What I would love to do is find a job where I could use this interest and earn a bit of money.
A Do you need a large salary?
B No, not really.
A In that case, you could think about working with disabled people. A lot of centres need, em, instructors, for example. You could get qualified as a sailing instructor.
B Mmm. That's interesting. Thanks.
A OK? Next caller, please.
C Good evening.
A Hello. How can we help?
C Well my problem is that I like my job but where I work there's not much chance of promotion. At least not for me.
A Why not?
C Well, the thing is I left school very young and I haven't really got any qualifications. People who joined after me are moving up but I'm not.
A Why did you leave school so young?
C Because I was bored.
A Mmm. Would you be prepared to do some training now?
C I suppose so.
A That's what I would recommend. Go to evening classes and get some qualifications to go with your experience. Thanks for calling. We've got time for just one more call and very quick, please. What's your question?
D I'm having problems with my boss.
A Oh, why's that?
D Well, my boss is my mother. I work for our firm as a salesman but she treats me like a child. I'm a good salesman and I'd like to prove myself by working for another company.
A Do it. Try the outside world for a couple of years but make sure the family business will take you back if you want to. It will be good for them as well to get some ideas from the outside world. Thanks for all your calls. Good night.

UNIT 5

5.1

1 Last year I bought a book about the painter, Degas from a local bookshop. When I got home I found the book was in Spanish not in English. I went back to the shop, but they didn't have the English version in stock. I asked for my money back and they said 'no'.
2 I booked a taxi to go to the airport to catch an early flight. The taxi arrived at my house almost an hour late and I missed my flight. I was furious! I certainly won't be using them again.
3 I bought a buggy for my baby by mail order and one of the wheels came off after just one week. I phoned the company to ask for a replacement. They said they would send one immediately. In the end it took nine phone calls and nearly two months to get a new one.
4 I bought a computer but didn't understand how to use the software so I called the after-sales support number. The person I spoke to was very unhelpful and made me feel really stupid. In fact he was very rude to me. That's the last time I buy anything from that company!
5 I'm going to start shopping at a different supermarket, because my supermarket doesn't offer its regular customers any reward for shopping there, but other supermarkets do.

5.2

1
A Last year I bought a book about the painter, Degas from a local bookshop. When I got home I found the book was in Spanish not in English. I went back to the shop, but they didn't have the English version in stock. I asked for my money back and they said, 'no'.
B They should give refunds if they want to get repeat business.

2
C I booked a taxi to go to the airport to catch an early flight. The taxi arrived at my house almost an hour late and I missed my flight. I was furious! I certainly won't be using them again.
D They should make their service more reliable.

3
E I bought a buggy for my baby by mail order and one of the wheels came off after just one week. I phoned the company to ask for a replacement. They said they would send one immediately. In the end it took nine phone calls and nearly two months to get a new one.
F They should improve the quality of their goods and their after-sales service if they want satisfied customers.

4
G I bought a computer but didn't understand how to use the software so I called the after-sales support number. The person I spoke to was very unhelpful and made me feel really stupid. In fact he was very rude to me. That's the last time I buy anything from that company!
H They should really make sure that employees at their call centre are always polite to customers.

5
I I'm going to start shopping at a different supermarket, because my supermarket doesn't offer its regular customers any reward for shopping there, but other supermarkets do.
J They should give regular customers loyalty cards.

5.3

People were more loyal to sites which were personalized and easy to use. The least popular of all the sites were those with no customer service telephone number.

For women, security was more important than anything else when buying online. They were slightly less interested in price than men. Women also wanted better human contact through telephone helplines, and quicker registration procedures.
The older age groups were happier to buy from sites operated by the most well-known shops, and from those which had the shortest registration procedures.
The most popular ISPs in the UK were Freeserve, AOL, and BT Internet.

5.4

1

A I think we should do it now. What do you think?
B I think so too. What about you, Chris?
C I don't agree. I feel we should wait.

2

D I think it's too late to do anything now.
E Yes, I agree. How do you feel about this, Frances?
F Well, I take your point, but I don't think time is a problem.

3

G It's a little expensive, Helen. Don't you agree?
H No, I don't think so. The cost is lower than last time.
I Yes, that's a good point.

5.5

I arrived late at a hotel in Cambridge, Massachusetts, the night before an 8 a.m. training course. When I got to my room I realized that I didn't have my professional work shoes in my suitcase. All I had was a pair of boots for the cold weather. So, I went to the hotel reception for help.
It was after 10 p.m. The receptionist told me that the shops didn't open until 9 a.m. the next morning. 'Is there nothing that can be done?' I asked her. She thought for a minute, then said, 'What size are you?' I told her, and she came out from reception, showed me the shoes she was wearing, and said, 'Will these be OK?' I couldn't believe it. She gave me her own shoes and I was ready for my audience the next morning.

UNIT 6

6.1

It all starts when a potential customer phones us or emails us to make an enquiry about our products. We provide them with the information, then send them a quotation, normally within forty-eight hours, if they want a standard product. The customer then places the order, and we begin to process it. Obviously, we check first of all that the product or products are in stock, then we confirm the order with the customer and give them a delivery date. If they agree with the date, we package the goods, and ship them to the customer. Our customers can track the progress of their order at any moment, in real time, using our online tracking service. We then deliver the shipment to the customer, hopefully to the right address, with the invoice attached. We then ask them to pay the invoice within thirty days. Fortunately, most of them do.

6.2

Supplier BCS Systems. Customer Support. How can I help you?
Customer Hello. This is Felton Engineering. F-E-L-T-O-N. I'm calling about an order. I'd like to know when we can expect delivery.
Supplier Could I have the order number, please, madam?
Customer Yes, it's 156 / 17A.
Supplier One moment, please. I'll just check. Right, here it is. 156 / 17A, you said?
Customer Yes, that's right.
Supplier OK, we're going to deliver to you on Friday morning, that's the third of April.
Customer Have you any idea what time?
Supplier Well, it's the driver's first call. I think he'll probably get to you at about 8.00.
Customer Oh dear. Is it possible for him to come a little bit later?
Supplier No problem. I'll just change the delivery details. Between 10.00 and 11.00. Is that OK?
Customer That's fine. Thanks very much.
Supplier You're welcome. Thank you for calling. Goodbye.
Customer Goodbye.
Colleague Is everything OK, then?
Customer Yes, they wanted to deliver at 8.00 tomorrow, but I said it was too early.
Colleague So are they going to change it?
Customer Yes, they're going to come between 10.00 and 11.00.
Colleague Ah, that's good.

6.3

1

A Can you send them today?
B I'm afraid we don't have them in stock at the moment.
A Oh dear. When will you have them?
B I think they'll be here in the next day or two.
A Well, could you let me know when they arrive?
B Yes, of course. I'll give you a call.

2

C You didn't send us enough.
D Oh, I'm very sorry about that. How many did you receive?
C Twenty-five, but we ordered forty.
D I do apologize for the mistake. Shall I send you the rest today?
C Yes, please. If you could.

3

E I'm sorry, but we can't find your invoice. When did you send it?
F On the fifteenth of June. Then we sent a reminder on the fifth of July.
E I'll just check again. Just one moment, please.
F Uhm ... Shall I send you another copy?
E No, that's OK. I'm sure I can find it.
F Listen, I'll send you another copy today. Then could you perhaps send us a cheque before the end of the week?

(((6.4)))

A Thirty years ago, there was a lot of talk about the 'paperless office'. It was said that computer technology would reduce the need for paper at work. Is this in fact happening? Are we using less paper than before?

B No we aren't. And I don't think that the situation's going to change in the near future. Let me give you a few statistics. The average American company with $1 billion in sales produces eighty-eight million sheets of paper each year. That represents one to three per cent of its turnover.

A But that doesn't tell me very much. Are we using more paper than before, then?

B Yes, at present paper use is growing by six to eight per cent a year, and I believe this figure will continue to increase.

A So why, in this age of electronic communication, is the amount of paper increasing?

B Well, studies show that companies with email are printing 40% more documents than before. In other words, employees prefer printing copies of emails rather than just keeping them on their computer. And the Internet is also partly responsible for the increase. The average employee prints thirty-three Internet pages every day.

A Thirty-three. That's incredible. So you don't think there will ever be a paperless office?

B No, I don't think so. I think we'll see more and more documents, like invoices, order forms, and so on, sent by electronic means ...

A So we'll continue to see a reduction in the amount of snail-mail.

B Yes, absolutely. But I think that when the documents arrive at their destination, we'll continue to print them for a long, long time yet.

A So why do people have this love affair with paper?

B Well, firstly, paper documents are very portable – you can take them where you want – to your home, to a meeting and so on. You can also make notes on them, which isn't easy with an electronic document. And finally, people don't want to spend their whole day looking at a computer screen – this can be very tiring and of course it's not at all good for the eyes. For this same reason, I don't think electronic books will ever replace the real thing.

UNIT 7

(((7.1)))

a We do tests on prototypes of new products. We've got two laboratories and a large, open-plan office.

b I check budgets and monthly figures for the board.

c I manage a team at one of the plants. We run tests on finished products to check they are up to standard.

d I'm in the commercial division. I'm responsible for a team of representatives working in the southern region.

e I spend a lot of time on the telephone trying to get the best prices. I'm in charge of buying raw materials.

f I spend a lot of time interviewing. We only recruit 25% of the people we meet.

(((7.2)))

This slide shows our structure. At the bottom, here, you can see the eight departments, or business units as we call them. The units are linked to one of the three divisions. Sales and Marketing are part of the Commercial Division. Purchasing, Delivery, and Quality Control are part of the Production Division and the other three units: HR, R&D, and Finance are part of the Central Services Division here at head office. There are seven people on the Main Board. Two of the Board are executive directors: Larry Felton the CEO, and Jane Figgis the CFO. The other five are non-executive. The Main Board is responsible to the shareholders.
Here you have the heads of the three divisions: Commercial, Production, and Central Services. Laura Holby is responsible for the Commercial Division. The Central Services Division is the responsibility of John McLaren, and Dr Karl Cooper is in charge of Production.
In all we have 395 personnel working for us with seventy-five here at head office, eighty working in the Commercial Division and 240 in the plants. Now, before I go on, does anyone have any questions?

(((7.3)))

Employee On the ground floor we have our R&D department, and obviously the reception area where we are at the moment.
Visitor 1 Excuse me. How many people work here?
Employee About eighty in this building. Then we have about twenty sales representatives who are on the road most of the week. Please follow me.

Visitor 2 When did you move to this building?
Employee About two years ago.

Visitor 1 Are you recruiting at the moment?
Employee Yes, we are. We are looking for people to work in the Customer Relations Department.
Visitor 1 What are they responsible for?
Employee They deal with orders and after-sales services and also look after our key clients. Here we are, the HR Department. This is Carla Brookes. She's in charge of recruitment.

Visitor 2 What's your website address?
Employee www.kazoo.com. It's easy to remember, isn't it?
Visitor 1 The reps spend most days visiting clients, don't they? Do they often come here?
Employee Just one day a week, usually on Mondays.

Employee This is the CEO's office.
Visitor 2 Is he British?
Employee No, he isn't. In fact, he's German.
Visitor 1 But it's a British company, isn't it?
Employee Yes it is. Next door, as you can see, is where the money is. They receive and make payments ...

(((7.4)))

Good morning. For those of you who don't know me, my name is Johan Hedborg. I'm an analyst and I work for a business magazine here in Brussels. I'm here today to tell you a little bit about Chupa Chups, the Spanish confectionery firm, which over the last forty years has become one of Spain's great success stories.

As you can see from this overview slide my talk is in four parts. Firstly, I'm going to tell you a little bit about the history of the company, from its foundation to the present time. Then, I'm going to talk about the structure of the company. After that, I'll look at their international activity in terms of marketing and production. Finally, I'll talk about its sales performance over the last ten years. Is that all clear? OK. Shall we start?

(((7.5)))

Have a look at this slide. It shows some of the key years in the history of Chupa Chups, from 1958 here on the slide to 2002 down here. Can everybody see that? So, there have been some interesting events in this period. From a production point of view, 1967 was a key year. The company opened production facilities in Barcelona and Bayonne in south-west France. From a marketing point of view, 1969 was important. If you look here you'll see the logo. The famous artist Salvador Dalí contributed to the design of the new daisy-shaped logo for the company that year, and it is still in use. As you can see here, the company continued to expand internationally in the seventies and eighties and in 1994, just here, they launched an adult product, 'Smint' (sugar-free mini mints), which is today one of the most popular global confectionery brands. In the following year they had a great marketing event when the Russian cosmonauts on the MIR space station had Chupa Chups, which became the first lollipops in space. In the last few years the company has had a new president with Xavier Bernat taking over from his father, and then in 2002 the new organization of the company. Now, shall I move on?

(((7.6)))

This slide shows the growth of sales over the eleven-year period from 1991 to 2001. The vertical axis shows sales in millions of euros and the horizontal axis shows the years from 1991 here on the left to 2001 here. For the first ten years sales went up every year from 31 million in 1991, reaching 424 million in 2000. From 2000 to 2001 sales fell slightly. As you can see, in 1995 there was a huge increase from 111 to 188 million. This was the year after the launch of Smint. There was another large rise in 2000 from 329 to 424 million.

(((7.7)))

That brings me to the end of my talk. Thanks very much for listening – I hope it was useful for you. Does anybody have any questions?

(((7.8)))

1 Hello. Is that Glorious Garden Furniture? Could I speak to the person in charge of advertising?
2 Good morning. I've just received a package from you and one of the chairs is broken.
3 Hello there. Do you have any vacancies at the moment in your Accounts Department?
4 Good morning. I'm calling from Garden Magazine. I'd like to write an article about your company.
5 Hello. This is Barclays Bank. We received a payment from Russia this morning. Is it for you?

(((7.9)))

A When did you move to Colletta?
B We came on holiday in 1998 and then bought a flat here the following year.
A Why did you move here?
B We both wanted to find a workplace which was relaxing but which allowed us to work efficiently. I'm a graphic designer and my husband works in IT.
A Do you work at home?
B Yes most days. I have a lot of clients in London but the airport here is only about an hour away so if I have to fly there it's very easy.
A So how often do you fly to London?
B About once a fortnight.
A What's special about Colletta?
B As a workplace it is perfect. We're high up so the air is pure and the views are marvellous. The flats are beautifully designed and it's a really peaceful place to work.
A Do all your neighbours work here?
B A lot of them do. Some people work here for three or four days and then go to their company on the other days.
A Does everyone speak Italian?
B We all try to speak a little but the main language of the village is English.
A Is it a friendly place to live?
B Definitely. There are lots of places to meet up, at the restaurant or at the swimming pool. Because everybody walks everywhere there are more opportunities for meeting people in the streets.
A Sounds very nice. There must be some disadvantages, surely?
B Well. It's a little isolated, particularly in the winter.
A And life's quite expensive here, isn't it?
B Well, yes, it is. The flats cost about 250,000 euros but we save on office rental and commuting costs.
A So you'd recommend Colletta as a workplace, wouldn't you?
B Definitely.

UNIT 8

(((8.1)))

Guest Mmm. This place looks interesting. Great decor.
Host Yes it is. The furniture's nice. The food is pretty good as well.
Guest What sort of food do they do?
Host It's written on the board over there.
Guest Wow. There's a lot of variety. How many courses shall we have?
Host Let's have a starter and a main course.
Guest What is 'scampi' exactly?
Host It's prawns covered in breadcrumbs and fried. It comes with chips and salad.
Guest Oh, I don't really like seafood. Is there anything vegetarian?
Host Oh, how about a vegetable curry?
Guest Too spicy.
Host Ravioli?
Guest Too heavy.
Host Pasta of the day?
Guest What is it?

Host Let me ask. Excuse me?
Waiter Yes?
Host What is the pasta of the day?
Waiter It's a vegetable lasagne.
Guest That sounds nice.
Host And to start with?
Guest Something light. I'll have the Greek salad – without olives.
Host I'll have the soup. Now what about some wine? Red or white?
Guest I prefer white. How about you?
Host White's fine. Now. Where is the waiter?

8.2

1
Diner Could I have a table for three, please?
Waiter Certainly. Would you like to follow me?

2
Diner What do you recommend?
Waiter Everything is very nice. What sort of thing do you like?

3
Waiter Are you ready to order?
Diner Could we have a few more minutes?

4
Diner What is the soup of the day?
Waiter French Onion.

5
Waiter How would you like it cooked?
Diner Rare, please.

6
Waiter Who's having the fish?
Diner I am.

7
Diner Could I have a glass, please?
Waiter Certainly. I'll get you one.

8
Waiter Would you like to taste it?
Diner Yes, please. Mmm, very nice.

9
Waiter Anything else?
Diner No, that was lovely. Thank you.

10
Diner Could I have the bill?
Waiter Certainly, sir. I'll just get it.

8.3

A Where do you think we should take them?
B Benito's is good. I went there last week and it was excellent.
A How much is it a head?
B About €35–40.
A Including wine?
B No – wine is about €20 a bottle.
A Sounds good. What do you think?
C Why don't we go to that new seafood place – Chapter Two?
B Expensive, isn't it?
C Yes, I think so. It's about €70 a head.
A Plus wine?
B Yes, and the wine there is not cheap – it's about €30 a bottle at least! There will be five of us so if we choose Chapter Two, it will cost us about €400. Benito's will be about half that.
C If it's a nice evening, we'll be able to sit outside at Chapter Two.
A But if it rains it'll be nicer at Benito's – there's a great atmosphere.
C Which evening are we going?
A Friday I think.
C That's a pity. If we go to Chapter Two on Thursday, there'll be live jazz.
B There's a singer at Benito's nearly every evening.
A OK. Do we have to book at Benito's?
B You can't. But it won't be full if we get there for just after 7.00.
A What time does it open?
B Seven, I believe.
A OK. Let's go to Benito's, then.

8.4

1. If we choose Chapter Two, it will cost us about €400.
2. If it is a nice evening, we'll be able to sit outside at Chapter Two.
3. If it rains, it'll be nicer at Benito's.
4. If we go to Chapter Two on Thursday, there'll be live jazz.
5. It won't be full if we get there for just after 7.00.

8.5

Tom What about you, Michael, do you like the cinema?
Michael Yes, I do.
Tom What sort of films do you like?
Michael Action films – American ones usually.
Tom And you, Jessica?
Jessica I'm not very fond of the cinema. I prefer the theatre.
Michael What sort of plays do you like?
Jessica Classical plays usually. I can't stand a lot of modern theatre. What about you, Stella?
Stella I don't go out very much, but I like collecting DVDs.
Jessica What sort of things do you collect?
Stella Anything, really – I love Hitchcock, but I also quite like musicals.
Jessica Do you like reading?
Stella Yes, non-fiction. Biographies and things. I'm not very keen on fiction.
Jessica Oh, I love reading, especially poetry. What about you, Tom? What do you like doing?
Tom I'm a great sports fan. Football, cricket, golf – I really enjoy watching them.
Stella But not playing?
Tom No, not really. I prefer taking my dog for a walk.
Stella What sort of dog is it?

8.6

A OK. Let's now look at some concrete examples. As we said, it is very important to react well in difficult cultural situations. Could I have a volunteer, please? Thank you.

Now. Imagine you are in Finland. You are trying to do business with a well-known telecoms company. It would be great business if you could get it. It is November and the weather is sunny but extremely cold. Their Sales Director says to you. 'Would you like to come for a swim in the lake before lunch?' What would you say?

B I would probably refuse politely. I would say, 'Sorry, I didn't bring my swimming costume.'

A And if he didn't accept your excuse; offered to lend you a swimming costume, for example, what would you say?

B If he said something like that I would say, 'Some other time maybe.'

A OK. Another volunteer. Right. Imagine you are in Japan visting one of your best customers. You are invited to a karaoke bar. Your customer asks you to sing a song in front of a crowd of about one hundred people. What would you do?

C If they asked me to sing I wouldn't know what to say. I would be too embarrassed. I would say, 'I'd love to hear some Japanese songs.'

A Mmmm.

8.7

Isobel Hi, Simon. Thanks for coming. I wanted to discuss your marketing plans for next year.

Simon Thanks, Isobel. As you can see, we are trying one or two new things.

Isobel That's what I wanted to discuss. First of all, you've budgeted for £20,000 on the British Grand Prix.

Simon That's right. I want to invite our top five customers to the race.

Isobel Why?

Simon To show them they are important to us. I'm sure it will persuade them to stay loyal and possibly do more business with us.

Isobel It's a lot of money to spend on customers we already have.

Simon That's the reason why we are doing it. We spend thousands on advertising for new customers and sometimes forget about our old and trusted ones.

Isobel Then, in September you are going to spend £15,000 on a concert.

Simon Yes. The idea is to invite about fifty customers, fifty suppliers and fifty potential customers to a classical concert sponsored by ourselves. It's in a beautiful hall with a fabulous orchestra. They will love it and will connect a pleasant experience to our name. I think it's a really good idea.

Isobel I'm not convinced. Is it even ethical?

Simon What do you mean?

Isobel Well, it's a little like giving them a gift in order to influence their decisions.

Simon So? Everybody does it. In different ways. We are only really trying to say thank you. We are not offering to pay for their family holiday or arrange university places for their children. That might be seen as unethical. I think entertainment is a normal part of relationship marketing.

Isobel Mmm, OK. You've argued your case well. I'll allow £15,000 for the Grand Prix and £10,000 for the concert. Cut out the champagne maybe ...?

UNIT 9

9.1

A What kind of rules and regulations are there on advertising in Thailand?

B Well, first of all, there are certain rules on the use of foreign languages. We are allowed to show commercials from other countries on TV, but all the voices must be in Thai. And the same is true for all the words that appear on the TV screen, or on the packaging for products – they have to be in the Thai language too.

A What happens when you have commercials with songs? Songs by American singers or groups, for example. Do they have to be translated?

B No, not at all. Songs can be in English, or in any other language. So advertisers don't have to provide a translation.

A Are there any taboo subjects – things that you mustn't mention in advertisements?

B Yes, you aren't allowed to make reference to religion, or to the monarchy – there is great respect for the Royal family.

A Yes, of course. And what are the rules on advertising particular products? Can you advertise alcohol, for example?

B Yes, you can show commercials for alcoholic drinks on TV, but you aren't allowed to see them before ten o'clock in the evening. And the advertisements mustn't include pictures or scenes of people drinking.

A And what about cigarettes and tobacco?

B You can't advertise them at all – not on TV or radio, not in newspapers, nowhere.

A And is comparative advertising allowed?

B In Thailand, no. Of course, you can say what the benefits of your product are to the consumer, but companies mustn't make specific comparisons with their competitors.

9.2

1 You can't advertise alcohol on TV.
2 You can show alcohol adverts at the cinema.
3 Cigarette companies can advertise in newspapers.
4 You can't show cigarette commercials on TV.
5 Cigarette commercials can be shown at the cinema.
6 You can't compare your products with your competitors'.

9.3

Sonya Right. Thank you for coming today. Can we start? We're here today to discuss the new sales campaign in Central Europe. Edward, you're going to give us the sales targets a little later, but let's talk about advertising first. Anton, this is your field. Could you tell us about the advertising budget for this year?

Anton Yes, of course. To support the new sales campaign, we are going to spend more on advertising this year. Last year we spent 28 million out of a total budget of 30 million euros. This year we are increasing the budget.

Edward Sorry, I didn't catch that, Anton. Could you go over those figures again?

Anton Yes, sorry. Our budget for last year was 30 million euros, but we only spent 28.6 million. For this year we've decided to increase the budget to 35 million euros. We are going to use the extra money to increase the amount of outdoor advertising. As I said at the last meeting, the idea is to make more use of bus shelters and billboards.
Sonya Yes, that's definitely a good idea.
Anton OK, if we now look at the budget for Western Europe ...
Sonya Er, sorry Anton, that's not really on the agenda for today. Can we come back to that another time?
Anton Yes, OK. But I really do think we need to discuss Western Europe too, to make a comparison ...
Sonya OK, I think we've covered advertising. Can we move on to the next point? That's sales forecasts. Edward, go ahead.
Edward Right. We forecast a seven to ten per cent rise in annual sales for this year, and we want to set a similar target for the two following years. That's in the countries where we have a stronger presence.
Anton Sorry, Edward I'm not with you. Could you be more specific? Which countries are we talking about?
Edward That's mainly Poland, Hungary, and the Czech Republic.
Anton OK, thanks.
Edward We're going to recruit fifteen new sales reps for these three countries, and we think ...
Anton Fifteen! Are you sure you've budgeted for that? Last year we ...
Edward Just a minute, Anton. Can you let me finish? I'm going to explain why we need so many people.
Anton OK, but I really don't see how we're going to ...
Sonya So, is there anything else?
Anton Well, as I said before, I really feel we need to review the budgets for Western Europe.
Sonya OK Anton, I agree, but I think we should have another meeting about that on another day. But I think that's everything for today. Can we sum up what we've agreed? Edward, you're going to prepare a detailed sales forecast, country by country, and Anton, you're going to ...

9.4

A Do you spend a lot of time in meetings then?
B Yes, I do. Probably about ... fifteen to twenty hours a week, I would think. What about you?
A Well, it's getting better. We've started a thing called the 'five-minute meeting'. All the project teams have them.
B That sounds like my kind of meeting. So does it really only last for five minutes then?
A Well, that's the theory. In practice it sometimes goes on for as long as forty-five minutes, but at least that's better than two or three hours, which was the case before.
B How often do you have those then?
A Every day, at two o'clock. There are six of us in each project team, and we all meet up in the team leader's office and discuss progress on the project.
B So do you have an agenda?
A No, not really. The five-minute meeting is just an opportunity to inform everybody of where you are in your work and to ask for advice on any little problems you're having. It works well.
B But why have a meeting at all? Why not just send an email to the team?
A Ah, well, with email, you often don't get the answer you want to your question. Only one person responds, for example, when you wanted everybody's opinion. Or they don't give you a complete answer so you have to write another email. It just takes too long.
B But just after lunch – isn't that the worst time of day to have a meeting? When we have meetings at that time, everybody's falling asleep.
A Well, that's difficult when you're standing up.
B Sorry, I'm not with you.
A Well, nobody sits down at our five-minute meeting. Not even the project leader. It's the best way to make sure that the meeting finishes quickly.
B So if I come to your office after lunch, I'll see lots of people standing around?
A Yes, that's right. Some visitors find it very funny – they ask if somebody's stolen the chairs or if we've got serious financial problems.

UNIT 10

10.1

So, how do we develop a new product? First of all, we decide on the different steps or stages in the development process. These include the writing of the program, testing it here in our centre, then in the client company, and so on. Following this, we prepare a provisional schedule for development of the product.
This brings me to the next stage. Now we go back to the customer and we agree on a deadline for delivery. This can be difficult – they often want it within two or three months, but we think it'll take six to twelve. But we always agree in the end! After that, we start developing the product. At the end of each week, we review progress on the project.
We keep a written record of all delays in the schedule, with the reasons for each delay. We deliver the product to the customer. Then finally, three months after delivery, we evaluate the success of the development project in a meeting with the customer and the rest of the project team.

10.2

A Yes, I got your email, but I'm not sure I understand. How does it work exactly?
B Well, it all starts when you receive some messages at your Spam-biters address, say fredsmith@spam-biters.com. First of all, the messages are checked for viruses. When this is done, the reject list is reviewed to see if the sender's address is on there.
A The reject list?
B Yes, that's the list of addresses you don't want to receive email from.
A OK, I see.
B OK. After that, the same thing is done for the contact list. If the address of the sender is included in your list of approved contacts, the message is sent directly to you, Fred Smith, and you can read it.

A Right, I'm with you. So what happens to the other messages – the ones from addresses that aren't on your contact list?
B All the other messages are transferred to the 'Blocked email log'.
A What's that?
B That's just the list of rejected emails. And Spam-biters send that list, or log, to you as often as you want – every day, once a week, every month ...
A And I can decide if I want to receive them or reject them?
B Yes, that's right. And you can also add the senders' addresses to your reject list or contact list.
A Sounds good.
B Yes, it is good. So you can say goodbye to companies who send you spam every month, for example. Once their addresses are placed in your reject list, every new message from them is rejected every time.

10.3

A Can we look at progress on the SNT contract now?
B Yes, sure.
A Where are we on the final quality tests?
B We did them all yesterday, and everything's fine. It all worked perfectly – no problems at all. But as for the training day on the 12th of June, I'm afraid we're running out of time.
A What's the problem then?
B Well, we've already had to cancel two dates because operators were ill. And this week another operator is on holiday.
A Well, we need to get a move on. SNT want to start production the week after next.
B I know. Don't worry. I'll take care of it. I'll make sure we arrange something for next week.
A OK, good. Now, when are we installing the robot?
B Tomorrow morning. There's a team of three people going over there, including myself. But I'm not sure it's enough. Can you come along too?
A Well I'm rather tied up tomorrow – I've got meetings most of the day.
B OK, leave it with me. I'll see if I can find another technician to come with us.
A That would be great if you could. And what about the software? Have you had a chance to test it on the SNT server?
B Well, we did some initial tests last week, and there were one or two bugs in the system. So we need to do some more when the robot is installed. They have to be done before the end of the week really. Can you deal with that?
A OK, I'll go there on Friday morning.

10.4

1
A Listen, I must go. I've got an appointment in five minutes.
B Yes, of course. Well, thanks for everything. That's really helped me a lot. And it's been great to talk to you again.
A Yes, and you. I'll send you the list, tomorrow, OK?
B Great, thanks. Have a good weekend.
A You too. Speak to you soon.
B Yes, bye.

2
A Thank you for inviting me. It's been a wonderful evening.
B You're very welcome. I really enjoyed it too.
A And we must do this again.
B Yes, we must.
A How about next Thursday? Are you free then?
B Um ... I'm not sure the contract will be ready for next Thursday.
A It doesn't matter, the contract can wait.
B Well ... Gosh, is that the time? Sorry, I really must go. I've got a train to catch.

10.5

1 It's been a really useful meeting.
2 Thank you very much for having me.
3 I hope to see you again very soon.
4 Have a nice holiday!
5 It's getting late. I really must go.
6 See you again next year.
7 I really enjoyed today.
8 It was very kind of you to help me.

10.6

Interviewer So where do these speed dating events take place, Tom?
Tom Well, the companies usually rent a comfortable bar or a restaurant or ... er ... some other kind of meeting room.
Interviewer And what kind of age groups do they attract?
Tom Well, most of the events are for people in the ... uhm ... 25 to 30 year-old age range. But I believe there are now some events for the 35 to 40 group also.
Interviewer And how many people come to a speed-dating party?
Tom Typically, the organizers invite about 100 people. And these hundred people are divided into two groups of fifty, each with twenty-five men and twenty-five women.
Interviewer And each person gets to meet twenty-five people?
Tom Yes, that's right.
Interviewer So, how does a typical evening work?
Tom Well, the room is usually filled with tables and sofas and comfortable chairs, and each table is numbered. Then, when someone announces the starting time, one woman and one man go and sit down at each table. They then have three minutes to talk.
Interviewer So what do you talk about? How much can you say in three minutes?
Tom Well, they normally give us a list of possible subjects. Oh yeah, and we're not allowed to talk about the job we do.
Interviewer Why's that?
Tom Because it's too easy to get the wrong impression of people from their job. They want us to focus on the personality of the person, not their work or how much money they earn.

Glossary

UNIT 1

a **brand** /brænd/ *noun* a commercial name used by a company for itself or its products: *Big Mac is a brand of hamburger.* Also to **brand**, to choose the name of a product
a **budget** /bʌdʒɪt/ *noun* an amount of money to be used for something: *We have a budget of €1,000 to buy new chairs for the office.*
a **competitor** /kəmpetɪtə/ *noun* a company selling similar products to you. Also to **compete**, *Pepsi is a competitor of Coca-Cola.*
a **consumer good** /kənsjuːmə gʊd/ *noun* a product for normal life, e.g. books, TV
to **employ** /ɪmplɔɪ/ *verb* to give someone a job
an **employee** /ɪmplɔɪiː/ *noun* a person who works for a company
to **expand** /ɪkspænd/ *verb* 1) to become bigger 2) to move into a new market
to **found** /faʊnd/ *verb* to create (a company)
to **file** /faɪl/ *verb* to organize papers and documents so they are easy to find
to **improve** /ɪmpruːv/ *verb* to make something better: *We want to improve our sales results.*
to **lend** /lend/ *verb* 1) to give for a short time: *Can you lend me your pen for a few minutes?* 2) to give money which must be paid back in the future
logistics /lədʒɪstɪks/ *noun* the organization of moving products from one place to another
to **manufacture** /mænjufæktʃə/ *verb* to make something in large quantities, especially in industry
a **market** /mɑːkɪt/ *noun* a geographical area, or part of the population, where you can sell goods: *the European / children's market*
a **product** /prɒdʌkt/ *noun* what a company makes to sell to the public: *We sell more than 3,000 different products.* Also **to produce**
a **product range** /prɒdʌkt reɪndʒ/ *noun* a group of products sold by one company
to **recruit** /rɪkruːt/ *verb* 1) to find new employees for a company. Also **recruitment**, *a recruitment agency* 2) to give a job to a new employee
to **request** /rɪkwest/ *verb* to ask for (in a formal situation): *I'm writing to request some information about your hotel.* Also to make a **request**
a **retailer** /riːteɪlə/ *noun* a company with shops which sell directly to the public
the **sales** /seɪlz/ *noun* the money a company receives from selling its products: *Our annual sales are $30 million.* (= **the turnover**)
to **spend** /spend/ *verb* 1) to use money to pay for something: *to spend money on clothes* 2) to use time: *I spent half an hour reading the report.*
the **staff** /stɑːf/ *noun* all the people who work for a company
a **subsidiary** /səbsɪdɪərɪ/ *noun* a company that is owned by a bigger organization
successful /səksesfl/ *adj* having good results: *a successful businessman / product / company*
a **supplier** /səplaɪə/ *noun* A company which sells goods to another company: *We buy all our office equipment from the same supplier.*
temporary staff /tempərəri stɑːf/ *noun* employees who work for a short time for a company
the **turnover** /tɜːneʊvə/ *noun* see **sales**

UNIT 2

advertising /ædvətaɪzɪŋ/ *noun* using TV, radio, newspapers, etc. to tell people about products. Also to **advertise** on TV, radio
to **cost** /kɒst/ *verb* 1) to have a price: *The phone costs $100.* 2) to decide a new product's price
the **design** /dɪzaɪn/ *noun* 1) the look or appearance of a product: *The new VW has a very modern design.* 2) drawing plans for a new product. Also to **design**: *Yves Saint-Laurent designs clothes for women.*
to **develop** /dɪveləp/ *verb* to take a basic idea, product, etc. and to work on it: *We're developing a new sort of soft drink.*
familiar /fəmɪliə/ *adj* something you recognize
to **introduce** /ɪntrədjuːs/ *verb* to start selling a product for the first time (= to **launch**): *They introduced the FX49 in May.*
an **invention** /ɪnvenʃən/ *noun* a new idea / product that was never made before
to **launch** /lɔːntʃ/ *verb* see to **introduce**
the **packaging** /pækɪdʒɪŋ/ *noun* the paper, cardboard, plastic, etc. you find around a product when you buy it. Also to **package**, to **pack**
a **patent** /peɪtənt/ *noun* a document that shows who owns the idea of a new invention
a **project** /prɒdʒekt/ *noun* a large piece of work with a clear plan
to **promote** /prəməʊt/ *verb* to tell the public about a new product by advertising, or visiting customers, etc.
a **prototype** /prəʊtətaɪp/ *noun* a first example of a product, from which a final version will be developed
a **reputation** /repjuteɪʃən/ *noun* people's general opinion about someone or something: *Our sales team / products have a very good reputation with our customers.*
research /rɪsɜːtʃ/ *noun* looking for and finding information. Also to **research**: *we're researching new ways of producing drugs.*
software /sɒftweə/ *noun* computer programs
a **sponsor** /spɒnsə/ *noun* a person or organization that pays money to a sports team, sportsperson, and gets advertising at stadiums, on clothes, etc. Also to **sponsor**, **sponsorship**
a **stage** /steɪdʒ/ *noun* part of a project: *Stage one, stage two ...*
a **survey** /sɜːveɪ/ *noun* a study of people's opinions
to **take over** /teɪk əʊvə/ *verb* 1) to become the Managing Director or CEO of a company 2) to buy another company
to **test** /test/ *verb* to see if something works
a **trademark** /treɪdmɑːk/ *noun* a special name for a product. Only one company may use it (™)
a **trial** /traɪəl/ *noun* testing a new product on possible future customers

UNIT 3

in advance /ɪn ədvɑːns/ before
an **appointment** /əpɔɪntmənt/ *noun* a meeting arranged with another person: *I have an appointment with a customer / my doctor.*
to **attend** /ətend/ *verb* to go to (a meeting / a conference)
a **bill** /bɪl/ *noun* a paper showing the price to pay in a restaurant, hotel, etc.
to **board** /bɔːd/ *verb* to get on a plane
to **book** /bʊk/ *verb* to reserve (a hotel room, holiday)
to **check in** /tʃek ɪn/ *verb* to tell officials that you have arrived at an airport, hotel, conference, etc. Also a **check-in** desk
to **check out** /tʃek aʊt/ *verb* (in a hotel only) to say you are leaving and to pay your bill
a **client** /klaɪənt/ *noun* a customer, someone who pays for a service
a **colleague** /kɒliːg/ *noun* someone who works in the same company as you
a **connection** /kənekʃən/ *noun* when travelling on a plane and you have to change to another plane, the second plane is your connection: *It's not a direct flight from London to San Diego – I have a connection in New York.* Also used with trains
a **contract** /kɒntrækt/ *noun* 1) a paper agreement between two groups 2) the document you sign with your working hours, pay, etc. when you work for a company
delayed /dɪleɪd/ *adj* late (because of problems): *The plane was delayed by snow.* Also a **delay**
a **fare** /feə/ *noun* The price of a travel ticket: *The plane / train fare to Oslo is €150.*
a **flight** /flaɪt/ *noun* a journey by plane
a **gate** /geɪt/ *noun* the part of an airport where customers board their plane
to **greet** /griːt/ *verb* to say hello to someone
to **have a look round** /hæv ə lʊk raʊnd/ *verb* to walk around a company / building and see what is there
insurance /ɪnʃʊərəns/ *noun* paying money to protect yourself from future problems / accidents: *life / holiday / travel insurance*
an **interview** /ɪntəvjuː/ *noun* a meeting where someone answers questions about something. Also to **interview** someone (e.g. for a new job)
to **land** /lænd/ *verb* to arrive in a plane at your destination
luggage /lʌgɪdʒ/ *noun* bags, suitcases, especially when travelling
to **negotiate** /nɪgəʊʃɪeɪt/ *verb* to talk about a disagreement and try to find a solution
overseas /əʊvəsiːz/ *adj / adv* in other countries
a **platform** /plætfɔːm/ *noun* a part of a station where people wait for and get on trains
to **register** /redʒɪstə/ *verb* to inform officials of your arrival at a hotel, conference, etc.
to **rent** /rent/ *verb* to pay money to use something for a limited time: *to rent a car / flat*
a **return** (ticket) /rɪtɜːn/ *noun* a travel ticket to go and to come back: *Would you like a one-way or return ticket?*
a **safe** /seɪf/ *noun* A strong metal box to put valuable objects in
security /sɪkjʊərəti/ *noun* protection from danger: *To improve security, we've put video cameras above all the doors.*
a **security pass** /sɪkjʊərəti pɑːs/ *noun* a card that people use to enter a building where only certain people can go. It may have a photograph
to **show round** /ʃəʊ raʊnd/ *verb* to take a visitor on a tour of your company, town, etc.: *Can I show you round the company?*
to **sign in** /saɪn ɪn/ *verb* writing your name when you enter a building
single /sɪŋgəl/ *adj* for one person, e.g. *a single room / bed*
to **take off** /teɪk ɒf/ *verb* 1) to leave the ground (in a plane) 2) to become successful (Unit 10): *The idea really took off in the second year.*
a **timetable** /taɪmteɪbl/ *noun* a list of times for trains, planes, etc.
a **trip** /trɪp/ *noun* travel from one place to another, often including the time spent there, and the return journey: *a business trip*
to **vacate** /veɪkeɪt/ *verb* to leave (especially a hotel room)
a **videoconference** /vɪdiəʊkɒnfərəns/ *noun* a meeting where the people are not in the same room but speak through cameras and televisions

UNIT 4

altruistic /æltruɪstɪk/ *adj* helping other people, without thinking about yourself
annual leave /ænjuəl liːv/ *noun* the days you have as holiday from your job
an **application** /æplɪkeɪʃən/ *noun* a formal request for a job, usually in the form of a CV and letter. Also to **apply for** a job
an **appraisal** /əpreɪzəl/ *noun* a conversation with your boss, usually once a year, to discuss your work or progress
benefits /benɪfɪts/ *noun* 1) the advantages that come with your job: company car, health insurance, etc. 2) the advantages that a product has for the people who buy it (Unit 9)
a **break** /breɪk/ *noun* a short time in the day when you stop working: *a coffee / lunch break*
a **career** /kərɪə/ *noun* your professional life from start to finish

CV /siːviː/ *noun* a document with your name, address, education, work experience, etc. You send it to companies when you apply for a job
disabled /dɪseɪbld/ *adj* having a serious physical difficulty, used to describe people who can't walk or see, etc.
to **earn** /ɜːn/ *verb* to receive money for the work you do: *He earns a very good salary.*
facilities /fəsɪlɪtiːz/ *noun* buildings, equipment, etc. for a particular use, e.g. offices and sports centres
flexible working hours /fleksɪbl wɜkɪŋ aʊəʒ/ *noun* when workers can choose what time they start and finish work
to **give up** /gɪv ʌp/ *verb* to (decide to) stop doing something: *to give up your job / smoking*
hospital fees /hɒspɪtl fiːz/ *noun* money you must pay for medical help at a private hospital
maternity leave /mətɜːnɪti liːv/ *noun* time when a mother stops working after she has had a baby. She is paid for this time by her company
paternity leave /pətɜ·nɪti: liːv/ *noun* a short period of time away from work for men just after they have become a father
a **pension** /penʃən/ *noun* money you receive after you finish work, in old age
qualifications /kwɒlɪfɪkeɪʃnz/ *noun* a diploma, certificate from school, university, etc.
to **reimburse** /riːɪmbɜːs/ *verb* to pay back money. Also the **reimbursement** (of travel / hotel expenses, etc.)
to **relocate** /riːləʊkeɪt/ *verb* to move to a new job in a different place, but with the same company. Also (to ask for) **relocation** to a new town
to **resign** /rɪzaɪn/ *verb* to tell your company that you are leaving your job. Also to offer your **resignation**
to **retire** /rɪtaɪə/ *verb* to stop working at the end of your professional life. Also **retirement**: *The age of retirement is 65 in many countries.*
a **salary** /sæləri/ *noun* money you receive every month from your employer
a **shortlist** /ʃɔːtlɪst/ *noun* a list of candidates who will be interviewed for a job. Also to **shortlist**: *We've shortlisted four people for the new sales job.*
training /treɪnɪŋ/ *noun* courses you can take to learn how to do a job or how to do your job better
up-to-date /ʌp tə deɪt/ *adj* (more) modern
a **vacancy** /veɪkənsi/ *noun* a job in a company for which a person is needed

UNIT 5

action points /ækʃən pɔɪnts/ *noun* things that must be done after a meeting
advice /ədvaɪs/ *noun* opinions that someone gives about what action to take: *He gave me some useful advice about good places to eat.* Also to **advise**
after-sales support /ɑːftə seɪlz səpɔːt/ *noun* help for customers after they buy a product. They can telephone a call centre to receive this
an **agenda** /ədʒendə/ *noun* a list of points for discussion at a meeting
AOB /eɪ əʊ bi/ Any Other Business, used in the minutes of a meeting. This is the time in a meeting where people can discuss subjects that are not on the agenda
an **audience** /ɔːdiəns/ *noun* the people who listen to a presentation, concert, etc.
average /ævəridʒ/ *adj* describes the usual or middle number, person, etc. in a group. *The average of 4 + 5 + 3 is 4.*
a **call centre** /kɔːl sentə/ *noun* a telephone department where staff answer questions from customers
a **complaint** /kəmpleɪnt/ *noun* saying that you are not happy about something: *We have to make a complaint about the slow service!* Also to **complain**
to **conduct** (a survey) /kəndʌkt/ *verb* to do (a survey, research)
customer satisfaction /kʌstəmə sætɪsfækʃən/ *noun* the feeling of being happy about a company's products or services. Also to be **satisfied** (with a product, service)
to **deal with** /diːl wɪð/ *verb* to do something to solve (a problem)
a **discount** /dɪskaʊnt/ *noun* an amount of money taken from the normal price: *We can offer you a discount of 20%.*
dissatisfied /dɪsætɪsfaɪd/ *adj* not happy
FAQs /ef eɪ kjuːz/ Frequently Asked Questions, used on websites and leaflets as a quick way of answering common questions
ISP /aɪ es pi/ *noun* Internet Service Provider. A company that provides a network to other businesses
an **item** /aɪtəm/ *noun* one point for discussion on an agenda
loyalty /lɔɪəlti/ *noun* staying true and faithful to the same person, company, etc. *We like to encourage customer loyalty.* Also **loyal**, *a loyal customer*
a **loyalty card** /lɔɪəlti cɑːd/ *noun* a plastic card that companies give to their customers. Every time the customer buys something in the shop, they get points. They can later use these points as payment for shopping instead of money
to **meet needs** /miːt niːdz/ to give people what they want. *To keep your customers, you have to meet their needs.*
the **minutes** /mɪnɪts/ *noun* the written report of a meeting
to **order** /ɔːdə/ *verb* to ask formally for goods: *We've ordered three new computers.*
Also to place an **order** (for goods)
polite /pəlaɪt/ *adj* to be nice and respectful to other people, not rude
popular /pɒpjələ/ *adj* used, liked, etc. by a lot of people: *a popular product / politician*
a **proposal** /prəpəʊzl/ *noun* an idea or suggestion, particularly at a meeting: *I liked her proposal for a new canteen.* Also, to **propose**
a **purchase** /pɜːtʃɪs/ *noun* something that you buy, or the action of buying: *When the customer has decided, he makes his purchase.* Also to **purchase**
quality /kwɒlɪti/ *noun* how good a product is (high quality / low quality). Also **quality** *adj* very good: *We make quality cars.*
to **recommend** /rekəmend/ *verb* to say that you think that something is good: *I can recommend this restaurant.* Also to make a **recommendation**
a **refund** /riːfʌnd/ *noun* your money back for something that you have paid for but don't want to keep. Also to **refund** (someone's money)
a **registration procedure** /redʒɪstreɪʃən prəsiːdʒə/ *noun* giving information about yourself to join an organization or a website, especially online
reliable /rɪlaɪəbl/ *adj* 1) always works properly 2) something that always happens at the correct time
repeat business /rɪpiːt bɪznɪs/ *noun* orders from customers who use your company again and again
a **replacement** /rɪpleɪsmənt/ *noun* a product that is changed for a broken or badly-working purchase
a **respondent** /rɪspɒndənt/ *noun* a person who answers a survey / questionnaire
a **silver surfer** /sɪlvə sɜːfə/ *noun* an older person (60+) who uses the Internet
unreliable /ʌnrɪlaɪəbl/ *adj* 1) often does not work 2) often comes at the wrong time (early / late)

UNIT 6

to **apologize** /əpɒlədʒaɪz/ *verb* to say sorry. Also to make an **apology**
to **cancel** /kɑːnsəl/ *verb* to say that something you have arranged won't happen: *to cancel a meeting.* Also the **cancellation** of a meeting, event, etc.
to **check** /tʃek/ *verb* to make sure that something is correct or working well: *Can you check the statistics / this machine?*
to **confirm** /kənfɜːm/ *verb* to say again that you agree with something: *He phoned to confirm the date of the meeting.* Also to send / receive, etc. (a) **confirmation** of something
a **deadline** /dedlaɪn/ *noun* a final date when something must be finished: *The deadline for delivery is March 15th.*
to **deliver** /dɪlɪvə/ *verb* to take or send goods to a particular place. Also to make a **delivery**
an **election** /ɪlekʃən/ *noun* when a group chooses a leader, often a country choosing its government / leader
an **enquiry** /ɪnkwaɪəri/ *noun* a formal request for information. Also to **enquire** about something: *I'm phoning to enquire about your products.*
a **flow chart** /fləʊ tʃɑːt/ *noun* a diagram with arrows used to show actions in order
an **invoice** /ɪnvɔɪs/ *noun* a document asking for payment, usually between two companies
Also to **invoice**: *They invoiced us for the two new machines.*
a **payment** /peɪmənt/ *noun* money paid for something
portable /pɔːtəbl/ *adj* small and light enough to carry: *a portable phone / computer*
a **prediction** /prɪdɪkʃən/ *noun* saying what will probably happen in the future. Also to **predict**
to **process an order** /prəʊses ən ɔːdə/ to take a request for a product then record the request, and send the product
to **quote** /kwəʊt/ *verb* to give a price for a product or service before the customer decides to buy. Also to make / provide a **quotation**
a **reminder** /rɪmaɪndə/ *noun* a letter, note, etc. to tell someone again that they haven't done something: *When we didn't receive the payment, we sent a reminder.* Also to **remind** someone to do something
to **ship** /ʃɪp/ *verb* to send goods by rail, sea, road, etc. Also a **shipment**: *Your shipment will arrive the day after tomorrow.*
a **stay** /steɪ/ *noun* a short period living in a place: *How was your stay in New York?* Also to **stay** in a hotel / with friends, etc.
stock /stɒk/ *noun* finished goods which are ready to sell: *They don't keep much stock in the shop. The product is in stock / is out of stock.*
to **track** /træk/ *verb* to follow the progress of an order, usually by the Internet
to **waste time** /weɪst taɪm/ to make bad use of time: *We're wasting time here – can we talk about this subject another day?*
within /wɪðɪn/ *prep* inside, used to describe a period in which something must be finished: *Please answer this e-mail within 24 hours.*

UNIT 7

Accounts /əkaʊnts/ *noun* the company department which keeps and checks the financial details of the business. Also an **accountant** (person)
an **axis** /æksɪs/ *noun* one of two lines in a graph. The line along the bottom is the x-axis. The line going upwards is the y-axis
the **Board** /bɔːd/ *noun* the group of directors who manage the company
in **charge of** /tʃɑːdʒ əv/ to have official control of: *He's in charge of the Sales Department / finding new customers.*
confectionery /kənfekʃənri/ *noun* sweets and chocolates, candy
to be **divided into** /dɪvaɪdɪd ɪntəː/ separated into: *The company is divided into four business units.*
a **division** /dɪvɪʒən/ *noun* a part of a company, often a large part
downward /daʊnwəd/ *adj* going down, getting worse
a **fibre-optic cable** /faɪbə ɒptɪk keɪbl/ *noun* a very fast line used for telephone communication and the Internet
figures /fɪgəz/ *noun* numbers, statistics, e.g. *sales figures*
a **fitness centre** /fɪtnəs sentə/ *noun* a place where people exercise, possibly with a gym and a swimming pool
a **growth** /grəʊθ/ *noun* an increase in the size of something. Also to **grow**: *The company has grown from 100 to 150 employees.*
horizontal /hɒrɪzɒntl/ *adj* flat, not up and down
Human Resources (HR) /hjuːmən rɪsɔːsɪz/ *noun* the company department which deals with recruitment, training, etc.
IT /aɪ tɪː/ *noun* Information Technology, computers: *an IT technician / manager / department*
a **laboratory technician** /ləbɒrətrɪ teknɪʃən/ *noun* a worker in a special room where scientific experiments happen
a **lawyer** /lɔɪə/ *noun* a person who works in the law, on contracts, in court
Legal Department /liːgəl/ *noun* the company department which deals with contracts, big problems of non-payment, etc.
an **organization chart** /ɔːgənaɪzeɪʃən tʃɑːt/ *noun* a diagram showing the structure of a company

a **plant** /plɑːnt/ *noun* a factory, e.g. *a production plant*
a **presentation** /prezənteiʃən/ *noun* an organized talk on a subject, often using visual aids. Also to **present** the results, a new product
Production /prədʌkʃən/ *noun* the company department that deals with making things
Public Relations (PR) /pʌblɪk rɪleiʃəns/ *noun* the company department that explains and develops the image of the company with the public
Purchasing /pɜːtʃəsɪŋ/ *noun* the company department that buys equipment, stationery, etc.
Quality Control /kwɒlɪti kəntrəʊl/ *noun* the company department that makes sure products and work are good
a **representative** /reprɪzentətɪv/ *noun* someone who works in sales, a salesman or saleswoman. Also can appear as a **rep**
Research and Development (R&D) /rɪsɜːtʃ ən dɪveləpmənt/ *noun* the company department that makes new products and improves old ones
to be **responsible for** /rɪspɒnsəbl fə/ (= in **charge of**)
to be **responsible to** /rɪspɒnsəbl tə/ having as your boss: *The Training Manager is responsible to the Human Resources Director.*
a **rise** /raɪz/ *noun* 1) an increase 2) an increase in salary
Sales and Marketing /seilz ən mɑːkɪtɪŋ/ *noun* the company department that finds and keeps new customers. It also tells customers about products
to **share** /ʃeə/ *verb* to have / use something with other people: *I share an office with two other colleagues.*
a **shareholder** /ʃeəhəʊldə/ *noun* a person / company who owns part of a company
a **slide** /slaɪd/ *noun* a prepared visual aid (with text and / or diagrams) for use in a presentation
to **stay the same** /steɪ ðə seɪm/ not change
subsidized /sʌbsɪdaizd/ *adj* partly paid for by the company, government: *Our lunches at work / school are subsidized.*
a **table** /teɪbl/ *noun* an organized list of information
a **trend** /trend/ *noun* 1) a change (in habits, financial results, etc.) which takes a particular direction: *There has been an upward / downward trend in TV advertising in the last year.* 2) a line on a graph showing this particular direction
vertical /vɜːtɪkl/ *adj* upwards and downwards

UNIT 8

an **atmosphere** /ætməsfɪə/ *noun* the general feeling produced by a place: *There's a very friendly atmosphere in the restaurant / company.*
can't stand /kɑːnt stænd/ *verb* hate strongly: *I can't stand fish – it makes me feel ill.*
corporate entertainment /kɔːprət entəteɪnmənt/ *noun* taking clients or customers on social events to improve business relationships
a **course** /kɔːs/ *noun* One part of a lunch, dinner: *We had a three-course meal, with chicken and rice for the main course.*
a **curry** /kʌri/ *noun* a spicy dish from India
cutlery /kʌtləri/ *noun* a group word for knives, forks, and spoons
dairy /deəri/ *adj* made from milk, e.g. cheese, butter, yogurt
a **dessert** /dizɜːt/ *noun* the last part of a lunch or dinner, often a sweet dish
a **dish** /dɪʃ/ *noun* a particular kind of food, prepared in a certain way: *Lasagne is an Italian dish.*
don't mind /dəʊnt maɪnd/ *verb* used when you have no strong opinion about something: *I don't mind watching tennis, but I prefer playing it.*
to **entertain** /entəteɪn/ *verb* to receive visitors and give them food and drink, or take them to shows, sports events, etc. *We entertained our customers with a night at the opera followed by dinner.*
filling /fɪlɪŋ/ *adj* used to describe food that is quite heavy. After eating it you do not need to eat any more food
to be **fond of** /fɒnd əv/ to like something very much
to **fry** /fraɪ/ *verb* to cook in hot oil
greasy /griːsi/ *adj* describes food that has a lot of fat, and feels fat when you touch it
a **guest** /gest/ *noun* a person who is invited (to a restaurant, company, etc.)
healthy /helði/ *adj* good for you. Describes food with a lot of vitamins, minerals, etc.
inedible /ɪnedɪbl/ *adj* impossible to eat (because it isn't nice)
to **influence** /ɪnfluəns/ *verb* to have an effect on someone's opinion: *My parents influenced my decision to become a doctor.* Also to have an **influence**
an **in-tray** /ɪn treɪ/ *noun* an open box on your desk where new work is put
to **knock over** /nɒk əʊvə/ *verb* to accidentally push something downwards, or down to the floor. If you knock over a cup, all the liquid inside comes out
overworked /əʊvəwɜːkt/ *adj* having too much work to do
packed /pækt/ *adj* (of a room, restaurant, etc.) very crowded
a **price range** /praɪs reɪndʒ/ *noun* the different costs of a company's products
a **private viewing** /praɪvət vjuːwɪŋ/ *noun* an opportunity to see a gallery / museum / event where the public is not allowed in
to **roast** /rəʊst/ *verb* to cook meat / vegetables in the oven in fat or oil
spicy /spaɪsi/ *adj* hot, with a very strong flavour
a **starter** /stɑːtə/ *noun* the first part of a lunch or dinner
to **taste** /teɪst/ *verb* 1) to try a little quantity of food or drink to see if it is good: *This soup's very good – would you like to taste it?* 2) to have a good flavour: *The sauce tastes very nice.* Also **tasty**
under pressure /ʌndə preʃə/ the feeling of having too much work and / or not enough time: *He's under a lot of pressure because he has to complete the project this week.*
veal /viːl/ *noun* the meat from a baby cow
a **vegetarian** /vedʒəteərɪən/ *noun* a person who does not eat meat or fish

UNIT 9

an **amendment** /əmendmənt/ *noun* a change to an official report, document, etc. Also to **amend**
Apologies /əpɒlədʒiːz/ *noun* a line in the minutes of a meeting with the names of people who were not able to come to the meeting
a **banner advert** /bænə ædvɜːt/ *noun* publicity for a company or product on the Internet
a **billboard** /bɪlbɔːd/ *noun* a big poster advertising a product, often placed next to roads
a **brochure** /brəʊʃə/ *noun* a document of several pages which describes a company's products or services. It often looks like a magazine
a **campaign** /kæmpeɪn/ *noun* a long programme: *We have started a 12-week advertising campaign on TV and radio.*
a **catalogue** /kætəlɒg/ *noun* a magazine or book listing a company's products and prices
a **celebrity** /səlebrɪti/ *noun* a famous person from the world of sport, cinema, etc.
to **come back to** /kʌm bæk tə/ (in a meeting) to return to a point that was discussed before
a **commercial** /kəmɜːʃl/ *noun* publicity for a company or product on TV
comparative advertising /kəmpærətɪv ædvɜːtaɪzɪŋ/ *noun* when a company uses an advert to say their product is better than a competitor's
to **cover** /kʌvə/ *verb* to deal with or talk about (subjects for discussion in a meeting): *I think we've covered all the points.*
a **feature** /fiːtʃə/ *noun* (of a product) a special thing / part: *A feature of this new train is the automatic doors.*
a **field** /fiːld/ *noun* 1) an area of activity: *I work in the field of computers.* 2) someone's area of special knowledge
a **forecast** /fɔːkɑːst/ *noun* a prediction about the future, based on present or past results: *Our forecasts show that sales will rise.* Also to **forecast**
a **free sample** /friː sɑːmpl/ *noun* an example of a product which you give to people to try for themselves
the **general public** /dʒenərl pʌblɪk/ *noun* individual, private customers (not company clients)
a **leaflet** /liːflət/ *noun* publicity for a company or product, usually on one piece of paper which is folded
to **move on** /muːv ɒn/ *verb* to change or advance to the next point for discussion: *Can we move on to the next point?*
promotional /prəməʊʃənl/ *adj* used for advertising
a **proof of identity** /pruːf əv aɪdentɪti/ *noun* an official document (e.g. a passport) which shows who you are
sharply /ʃɑːpli/ *adv* changing a lot, very fast
slightly /slaɪtli/ *adv* by a very small amount: *Prices increased slightly by 0.1%.* Also a **slight** increase / decrease, etc.
a **slogan** /sləʊgən/ *noun* a short phrase used in an advertisement to help people remember the product or company
specific /spəsɪfɪk/ *adj* giving clear information, giving more detail: *I don't understand. Can you be more specific?*
steadily /stedɪli/ *adv* at a regular speed or rate: *Sales increased steadily by 2% a month for the first six months.* Also a **steady** increase / decrease, etc.
a **target group** /tɑːgɪt gruːp/ *noun* a group of customers that a company wants to attract
word of mouth /wɜːd əv maʊθ/ 'free' publicity where people tell family, friends, etc. how good a company or product is

UNIT 10

to **analyse** /ænəlaɪz/ *verb* to examine something in detail (results of tests, surveys, etc.) to learn something about it. Also to make an **analysis**
a **balance** /bæləns/ *noun* when two or more things are the same or equal: *To be happy in life, you need a good work-life balance.* Also to **balance** (work and home life)
a **contact** /kɒntækt/ *noun* someone you send emails to
energy levels /enədʒi levlz/ *noun* your ability to work because you are awake or tired: *I tried to write the project but I couldn't. I needed a coffee because my energy levels were low.*
to **evaluate** /ɪvæljueɪt/ *verb* (= to **analyse**) to say how good or bad something is. Also **evaluation**
an **impression** /ɪmpreʃən/ *noun* an effect that a person or thing has on you: *If you want to give a good impression to your customers, always arrive on time.*
an **interruption** /ɪntərʌpʃən/ *noun* something / someone that stops you while you are saying or doing something: *It's difficult to finish this letter because I have so many interruptions.* Also to **interrupt**
to **meet a deadline** /miːt ə dedlaɪn/ to finish something on (or before) the date fixed for finishing it: *We didn't meet the deadline of 15th July, and delivery was three days late.*
to **monitor** /mɒnɪtə/ *verb* to check or look at something regularly
provisional /prəvɪʒənəl/ *adj* not final, can be changed later: *I'm sending you a provisional programme for the conference for your comments.*
to **record** /rɪkɔːd/ *verb* to write down the details of something: *We record all customer complaints in a special book.* Also (to keep) a **record** of something
to **reject** /rɪdʒekt/ *verb* to say something is not good enough and should not be used
to **review** /rɪvjuː/ *verb* to look at something again
to **run out of** /rʌn aʊt əv/ *verb* to stop having enough of something you need
a **schedule** /ʃedjuːl/ *noun* a plan of visits, events, meetings, etc. with times and / or dates. Also to be **behind schedule** (= late with a project), **on schedule** (= on time), **ahead of schedule** (= finishing a project early)
a **step** /step/ *noun* one part of a process
to **take care of** /teɪk keə əv/ (= to **deal with**)
a **task** /tɑːsk/ *noun* a piece of work to be done
to be **tied up** /bi taɪd ʌp/ to be too busy to do something: *I can't come to the party tomorrow, I'm a bit tied up*
to **transfer** /trænsfɜː/ *verb* to move people, documents, data, etc. from one place to another

OXFORD
UNIVERSITY PRESS

Great Clarendon Street, Oxford OX2 6DP

Oxford University Press is a department of the University of Oxford. It furthers the University's objective of excellence in research, scholarship, and education by publishing worldwide in

Oxford New York

Auckland Bangkok Buenos Aires Cape Town Chennai Dar es Salaam Delhi Hong Kong Istanbul Karachi Kolkata Kuala Lumpur Madrid Melbourne Mexico City Mumbai Nairobi São Paulo Shanghai Taipei Tokyo Toronto

First published 2004

ISBN 0 19 4379752

Printed in Hong Kong

Acknowledgements

The authors and publisher are grateful to those who have given permission to reproduce the following extracts and adaptations of copyright material:

pp 12–13, 128 'Heinz marketing aims green ketchup at little squirts' by Patricia Sabatini, copyright *Pittsburgh Post-Gazette* 10 July 2000, all rights reserved. Reproduced by permission.

p 20 'Videoconferencing expands', copyright *USA Today* 10 June 2000. Reproduced by permission.

pp 27, 130–131 Brazil: Travel Advice and Social Customs from www.tradepartners.gov.uk. Reproduced by permission of Her Majesty's Stationery Office.

pp 30–31 Adapted extracts from 'How to use career skills to follow your passions' by Joann S. Lublin, *Wall Street Journal* (online). Reproduced by permission of the Copyright Clearance Centre.

pp 38–39 'In search of bargains' by Kate Quill © Times Newspapers Limited 15 January 2001. Reproduced by permission.

pp 43, 133 'Creative Customer Service – How far will you go to wow a customer?' by Mary Sandro, © *Professional Edge*. Reproduced by permission of Mary Sandro.

pp 56–57, 98, 134–135 Information about Chupa Chups. Reproduced by permission of Chupa Chups S.A.

p 69 Information about Kodak Advantix Preview camera. Reproduced by permission of Kodak Limited.

Although every effort has been made to trace and contact copyright holders before publication, this has not been possible in some cases. We apologize for any apparent infringement of copyright and if notified, the publisher will be pleased to rectify any errors or omissions at the earliest opportunity.

Sources

p 5, 127 www.hoover.com (Candy)

p 6 www.gapinc.com

pp 14–15, 85, 93, 128 www.xerox.com

p 15 www.americanheritage.com

p19 *Business Week*, 6 August 2001 (Brand Value)

p 44 www.ec.ups.com (UPS and MisterArt)

pp 59, 135 www.colletta.it, *The Guardian* September 2001, *Daily Telegraph* March 2002 (Colletta)

pp 70–71, 137 www.asianmediaaccess.com.au (Information about Thailand, Sri Lanka and Japan)

p 83 www.hurrydate.com

pp 102–103 www.publishers.org.uk, www.ipa-uie.org, www.fipp.com/data (Book and magazine spending trends)

The authors and publisher are grateful to the following individuals who read and piloted the material:

Nick Barrall, Martin Bradbeer, Mark Dudley, Manuela Escobar Montero, Claire Giffen, Beáta Harmati, John Hughes, Rebecca Kirby, Ian Lawrence, Mike McDevitt, Paul McMahon, Bill Porter, Joanna Westcombe

The publishers would like to thank the following for the use of photographs and copyright material:

Advertising Archive Ltd pp 6, 14; ©Archivo gráfico. Telefónica S.A. p 4 (car); ©Buitoni p 4 (pasta); ©John Chen p 30; ©Chupa Chups pp 56, 98; ©Colletta/Realinvest Ltd p 59 (colletta); CORBIS p 15 (©Roger Reemeyer), p 19 (SYGMA/©Van Parys), p 20 (©Steve Chenn), p 58 (©Charles Gupton), p 67 (©Steve Raymer/theatre), p 76 (©Dave Teel); GettyImages/Imagebank p 16 (Britt Erlanson), p 27 (Larry Dale Gordon/people), p 35 (Jeff Cadge), p 36 (Tom Hussey) p 38 (John William Banagan / shopping, Rob Atkins / trolley), p 44 (Larry Gatz / courier), p 60 (Sean Justice / sandwich, China Tourism Press / business lunch), p 63 (Andrea Pistolesi / table setting, Barros & Barros / chef), p 68 (Ulf Wallin), p 75 (Larry Dale Gordon / hotel); GettyImages / PhotoDisc Collection p 49 (agnetha, bernard); GettyImages / Photographers Choice p 36 (Yellow Dog Productions / queue); GettyImages / Stone p 21 (Bob Thomas / travel agent, Christopher Bissell / check-in, Steven Peters / reception), p 59 (Frank Herholdt / male), p 63 (Janusz Kawa / two women), p 67 (Oli Tennent / racecourse); GettyImages / Taxi p 7 (V.C.L), p 27 (V.C.L / mountain), p 49 (Andreas Pollok / mario, Bay Hippisley / chloe), p 67 (V.C.L / hot air balloon), p 70 (Karin Slade), p 75 (V.C.L / Spencer Rowell / walk, CHABRUKEN / stand); 'Courtesy of Heinz North America', pp 12, 13; ©Hong Kong International Airport p 86; ©Hoover Candy Group p 5; ©Hotel Alfonso XIII p 94; ©Kodak p 69; ©L'Oreal p 4 (shampoo); ©Muji p 4 (shop); ©Porsche p 4 (production line); Rex Features p 83 (Richard Saker); ©Sainsbury p 44 (food delivery); Photodisc p 53 (larry felton, jane figgis, karl cooper, john mclaren); Stockbyte p 53 (laura holby).

Illustrations

Francis Blake pp 32, 72; Kate Charlesworth pp 24, 47, 50, 82; Bob Dewar pp 17, 28, 40, 61; Mark Duffin p 54; Helen Flook pp 11, 43, 46, 65; Royston Robertson pp 8, 52, 64, 81.